# RAILROADS

## of Southeast Iowa

### Photographs from
### The Lemberger Collection

PBL Limited
Ottumwa, Iowa

**Railroads of Southeast Iowa**
**Photographs from The Lemberger Collection**

Copyright 2012 by Leigh Michaels & Michael W. Lemberger

Cover and design copyright 2011 by Michael W. Lemberger

This edition published 2012

10  9  8  7  6  5  4  3  2  1

ISBN :   1-892689-91-X
ISBN 13:    978-1-892689-91-7

Printed in the United States of America

Illustrations courtesy of **The Lemberger Collection**.  For more information about the collection, which has been called the largest and best-documented privately-owned photography collection in the world, see www.mlemberger.com

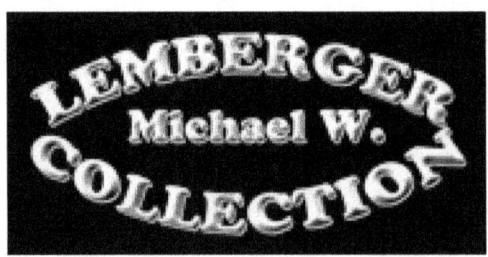

All rights reserved. Except for brief passages quoted in any review, the reproduction or utilization of this work in whole or in part, in any form or by any electronic, mechanical, or other means, now known or hereinafter invented, including xerography, photocopying and recording, or in any information storage and retrieval system, is forbidden without the express permission of the publisher.
For permission contact:
    Rights Editor
    PBL Limited
    P.O. Box 935
    Ottumwa IA 52501-0935
    pbl@pbllimited.com

Visit our website at www.pbllimited.com for more information about this and other publications. Quantity and wholesale prices are available.

Burlington Engine #1, The Pioneer

In memory of Edwin D. Lemberger
1906-1983
Brakeman, union leader, politician, postmaster
-- and Dad

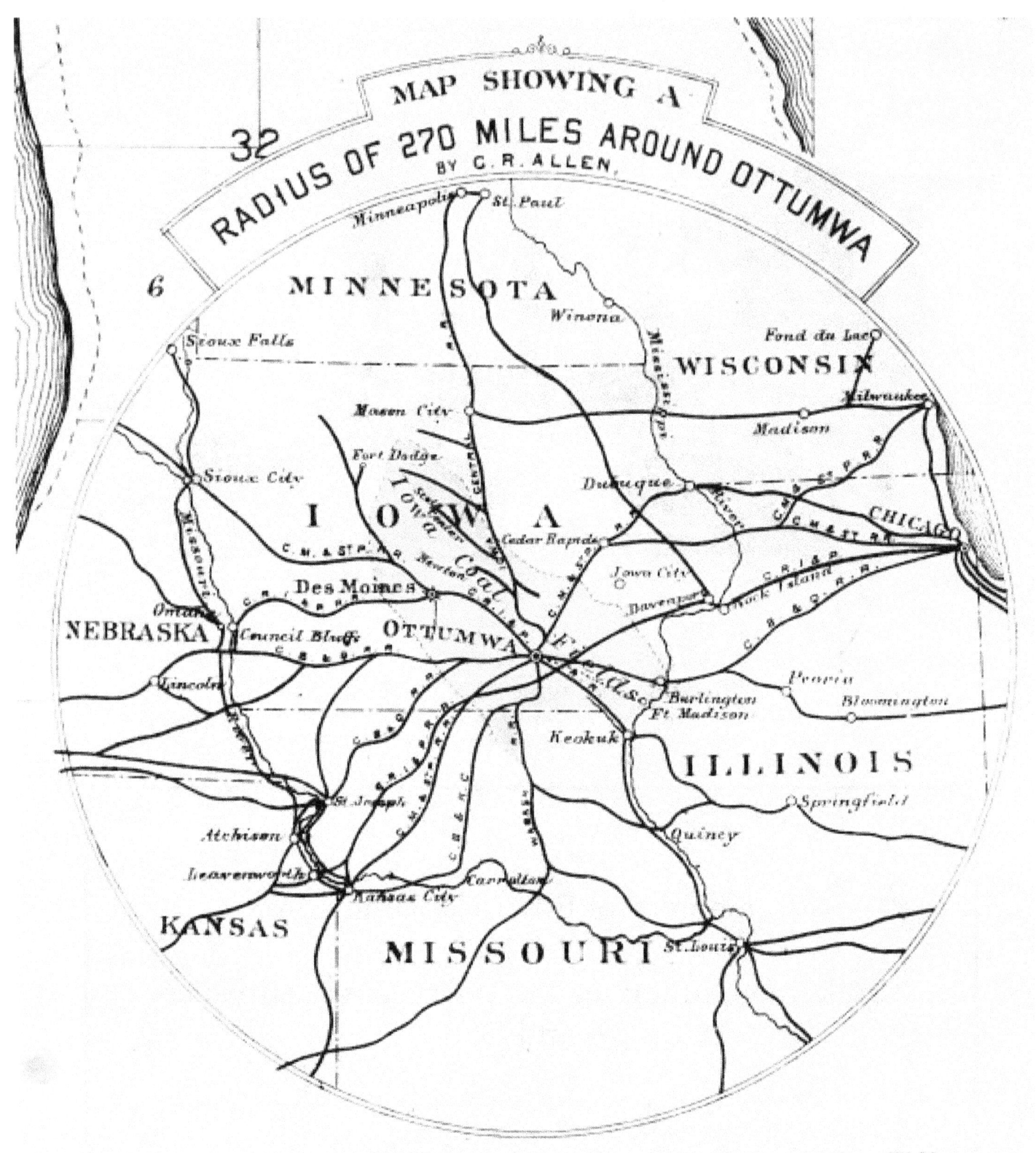

This 1891 map shows railroad lines for a 270 mile radius around Ottumwa. In the 1890s, Ottumwa was served by five separate railroad lines -- the C.B. & Q, the C.R.I. & P., Wabash Western, C.M. & St.P., and Iowa Central.

# A Word from the Editors

Though early settlement in Iowa followed the rivers, it was the advent of
the railroads, starting in the late 1850s, which opened up the remainder
of the state for development -- bringing goods to residents
and sending their crops and products out to the world.
Railroads formed the backbone of middle America,
with dozens of trains -- freight and passenger -- reaching out to
nearly every small town in the region.

This book is not intended to be a history of the many railroads
which operated in Southeastern Iowa
from the mid-19th century to the present.
Our goal instead has been to provide snapshots in time.

Our thanks go to Bill Greenley (retired engineer for the Milwaukee, Soo,
CP, IMRL, and Amtrak lines) for his tireless assistance.
Thank you to R E. Boyd (retired engineer for the Milwaukee),
Larry Lynch (retired engineer for the Rock Island and Soo),
Monte King (retired engineer for the Milwaukee),
and Chuck McElroy (retired yardmaster for the Milwaukee)
for the valuable information and depth which they added.

Thanks also go to Michael W. Lemberger's Facebook group,
who provided background, research, and support for this project.

Photographs courtesy of the Lemberger Collection.
Photographer and archivist Michael W. Lemberger
began collecting images at the age of eight
when he discovered a cache of glass negatives in his great-aunt's attic.
In the next 60 years he amassed more than a million images,
including his own photographs and those of other professional
and dedicated amateur photographers. The Lemberger Collection
(see www.mlemberger.com for more information)
has been called the largest and best-documented privately-owned
photography collection in the world.

# Railroads of Southeast Iowa

Steam engine in front of Rock Island depot, Ottumwa, 1800s.

# 1865. EASTWARD. 1865.

## DES MOINES VALLEY,
## Burlington & Missouri River
### AND

## CHICAGO, BURLINGTON QUINCY
### RAILROADS.

### SHORT & QUICK ROUTE TO THE EAST
FROM ALL POINTS IN SOUTHERN AND WESTERN IOWA.

BE SURE AND PURCHASE TICKETS VIA

# BURLINGTON

Two Trains Leave PELLA Daily on the arrival of Stages from DES MOINES, connecting at Ottumwa with Trains for

## BURLINGTON AND CHICAGO!

TICKETS FOR SALE BY THIS ROUTE AT
### OMAHA, NEBRASKA CITY, LEWIS, DES MOINES, PELLA & OTTUMWA

BAGGAGE CHECKED THROUGH FROM OTTUMWA TO

# CHICAGO
Close Connections made with the GREAT TRUNK LINES leading East, North and South

### SLEEPING CARS ON ALL NIGHT TRAINS.

Passengers will find this route Quick, Safe and Sure in its Connections

L. CARPER,            C. E. PERKINS,
General Freight and Passenger Agent, Burlington, Iowa.     Superintendent B. & Mo. R. R. R.

J. B. FLAGG, General Agent, Ottumwa.

# Railroads of Southeast Iowa

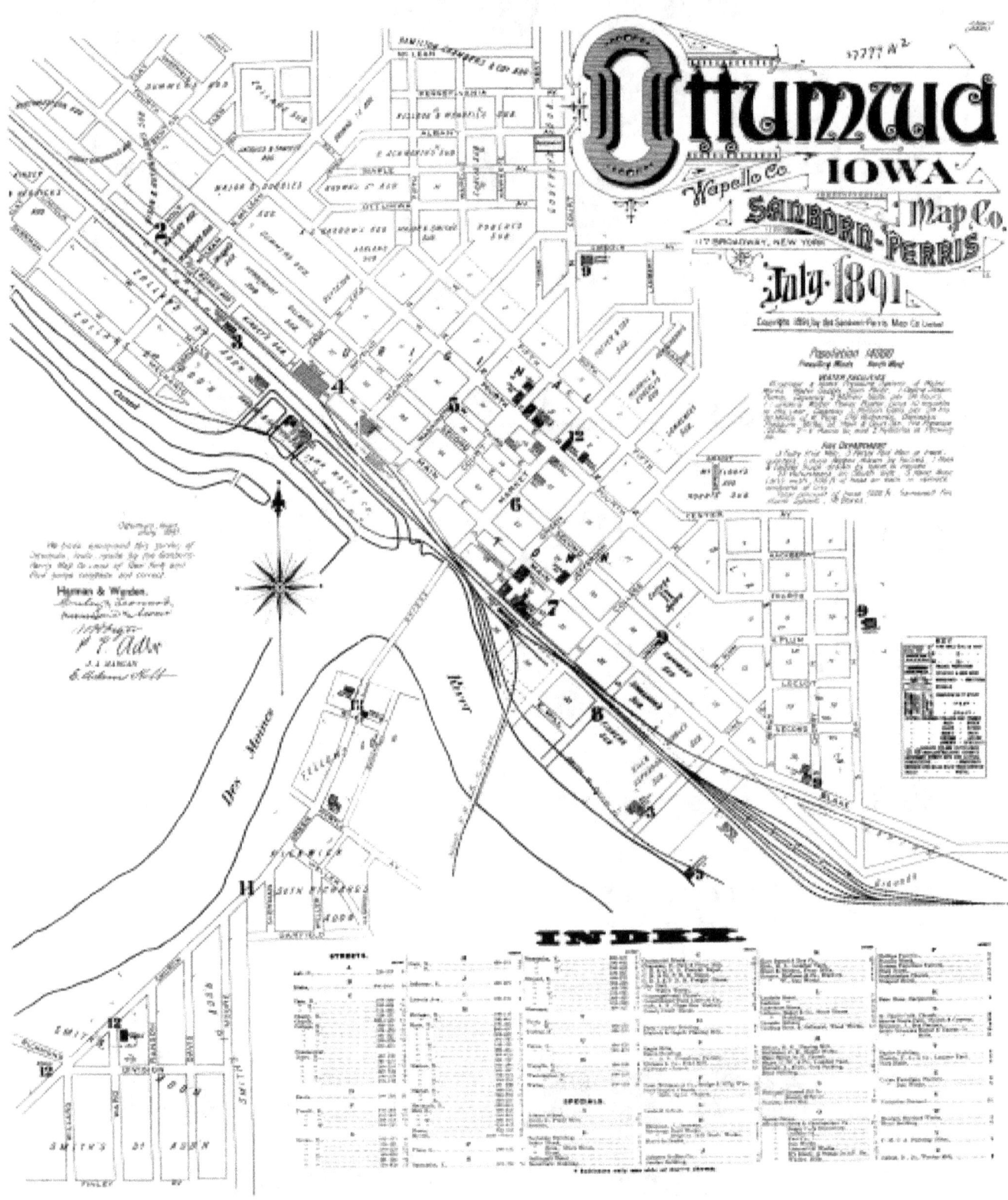

# The Lemberger Collection

The 1880s or 1890s -- Engine # 44 with crew.

Four coal-burning Mogul steam engines lined up in front of Union Depot in Ottumwa in the 1800s.

# The Lemberger Collection

Moguls were heavy-duty passenger or freight engines, with a configuration of 2-6-0 -- two pony wheels at the front, six drive wheels, and no trailers.

C. B. & Q. Railroad handcar and section crew in the 1800s. A section crew maintained a portion of track, usually several miles in length.

## The Lemberger Collection

Wabash Railroad Depot in South Ottumwa, before 1900.
The exact location of this station is not known, but it is thought to have been just south of the river, a block or two from
where the Jefferson Street Viaduct now ends.

# Railroads of Southeast Iowa

Union Depot, Ottumwa, 1800s.

# The Lemberger Collection

C.B. & Q. Depot, Agency, Iowa.
The pole behind the depot was a railroad semaphore used to give orders
to oncoming trains before radios were available. The double arm of the semaphore
could give separate orders to two engineers on two trains; each obeyed the arm
which -- seen from his position -- extended to the right of the pole.
The downfacing arm seen at the right is a sign to the engineer that he may proceed.
The straight-out arm to the left is a signal for an oncoming train to stop.

Believed to be the
trestle bridge carrying
a narrow-gauge railroad
line which ran through
Rubio, Martinsburg,
and Oskaloosa and on
to Des Moines.
(another photo next pages)

# Railroads of Southeast Iowa

1800s -- Railroad Bridge under construction, showing the work crews, horses and equipment. This bridge was built for the Northwestern Railroad by Ralph C. Ream. While the exact location is not known, the bridge is thought to have been located north of Hedrick.
The trestle bridge at left carries a narrow-gauge line running through Rubio, Martinsburg, and Oskaloosa to Des Moines.
The Northwestern Railroad later merged with several other roads and became the Union Pacific.

# The Lemberger Collection

Horse drawn equipment working on the hill included scrapers, the earth-movers of the day. Sheep were used to tamp the dirt down after fill was moved into place. The animals were held to one side of the area until tamping was needed, then feed was placed for them on the other side of the track so their small hooves would pound the dirt into place as they passed.
At the bottom on the right side of the photo are an axe grinder and a water trough. One worker would be assigned to sharpen tools -- his only job -- while his assistant ferried newly-sharpened tools to the workers and brought back dull ones.

Diamond Stack steam switch engine #236, photographed in downtown Ottumwa in the 1800s. This coal-fired engine had a 0-4-2 configuration (no pony wheels, four drive wheels, two trailers). Note the very large headlight on top of the wooden cab, at the back. The small protrusion at the top front of the cab was the whistle.
To connect cars, this type of engine used the link-and-pin system, which was the source of many a brakeman's injuries -- he had to lift the link, drop in a pin, and pull his hand out, all while the engine was in motion. This engine was hand-fired, carrying a fireman who shoveled coal into the firebox.

# The Lemberger Collection

Union Depot in Ottumwa in the 1880s, with a steam locomotive passenger train in front. This was an American engine with a 4-4-0 configuration. The first car behind the tender was a combine car (combination passenger and freight car) with two passenger coaches behind. The back half of the tender was usually a water tank, with coal stored in the front half, where it would slide toward the engine.

January 15, 1888 -- two trains collided head on, four miles west of Ottumwa. Though the railroad line is not known, the car at right was part of the Rock Island.

# The Lemberger Collection

Most of the casualties among engine crews in this era were from either crush or burn injuries. As a tender crashed into the locomotive, crews would often be trapped, only to be scalded as the firebox and boiler ruptured.

# Railroads of Southeast Iowa

Union Depot and railroad lines, photographed in 1890.
The narrow water channel pictured above, known as The Race, was a small side channel of the the Des Moines River, created in 1875 to produce hydroelectric power for the city. It was later filled in as part of

# The Lemberger Collection

the river-straightening project. Though the depot appears to have two towers, the dome-shaped tower to the left is actually that of the Coal Palace, which was located north and west of the depot. The pointed tower at the right is atop the depot. It was removed in the 1950s renovation.

# Railroads of Southeast Iowa

On September 15, 1891, Congressman William McKinley (later President McKinley) arrived by train in Ottumwa to speak at the Coal Palace during its second season. McKinley is thought to be the man at bottom center with his hat in hand.

C. B. & Q. passenger depot -- Albia, Iowa (Monroe County)

# The Lemberger Collection

Humeston depot, Humeston, Iowa (Wayne County) where two railroads crossed. The depot is L-shaped so each railroad had a separate entrance.

# OTTUMWA'S NEW RAILWAY.

## The Chicago, Ft. Madison & Des Moines R'y.

The Chicago, Ft. Madison and Des Moines Railway, Recently completed between Ft. Madison and Ottumwa, forms one of the shortest and quickest routes between the east and south and Ottumwa. Passengers for Chicago and St. Louis and all points beyond, will find that the new route has many advantages.

The Chicago, Ft. Madison and Des Moines Railway is the Fast Freight Line between Ottumwa and the east and south. Through Merchandise Freight Service having been established with its eastern connections. When ordering goods from Chicago and the east instruct shippers to route "via Santa Fe and C., F. M. & D. M."

For rates, tickets and further information apply to agents of Chicago, Ft. Madison, and Des Moines Railway, or address ———

E. F. POTTER,
GENERAL SUPERINTENDENT.

J. C. MACKINNON,
General Freight and Passenger Agent.
FT. MADISON, IOWA.

View of Ottumwa from the tower of the Union Depot, during the 1890s. This view looks east toward Adams School, visible on the horizon

## The Lemberger Collection

(site of the present-day Ottumwa High School). The intersection shown just beyond the construction site is Main and Court.

In 1898, a group of Iowa soldiers embarked at the Wabash Railroad Depot in Ottumwa, on their way to fight in the Spanish-American War. Note the dog sitting on the horse's back.

**The Lemberger Collection**

The depot was located on the north side of the river, near the end of the railroad bridge leading to Dain Manufacturing (John Deere Ottumwa Works), and near the present site of the Jefferson Street Viaduct.

# Railroads of Southeast Iowa

Looking northward across the Des Moines River, before 1899. The Wabash bridge ran from Dain Manufacturing (later John Deere Ottumwa Works) to the main rail lines. It is now part of a bicycle and walking trail. The tower of the Wapello County Courthouse is visible on the horizon to the left.

## The Lemberger Collection

The smokestack at center is part of Iowa Southern Utilities' downtown generating station. It was removed in the 1970s. The cupola atop the Wabash Depot is visible just to the left of the bridge. The building on stilts next to it was the car shop where railroad cars were repaired. Arthur McElroy was the car shop foreman.

# Railroads of Southeast Iowa

The railroad yards just east of the Union Depot in about 1900. Only two tracks now remain in this area. Smokestacks of the Iowa Southern Utilities downtown generating station are in the background. Warehouses to the left have been replaced by new commercial development. The Race lies immediately to the right of the tracks, crossed by the Milwaukee bridge

# The Lemberger Collection

(closest to the camera). Beyond the Race, the Des Moines River sweeps around a bend and under the Market Street bridge -- the river would not be straightened for another 50 years. The bridge in the distance is the Wabash bridge leading to Dain Manufacturing. The Jefferson Street Viaduct was not yet built.

By about 1900, underbrush had grown up along the banks of the Race, next to Union Depot.

*(Right, bottom)* The Milwaukee Railroad bridge over the Race, looking upstream toward Union Depot (the tower in the background). The present hydro dam across the Des Moines River is roughly in the same location as the bridge.
The school building on the horizon was Ottumwa High School at the time; it later became Washington Junior High and the building burned in 1990.

# The Lemberger Collection

The south leg of the Milwaukee Railroad Wye bridge spans the Des Moines River north and west of Union Depot. Sherman Street depot is in the background.

# Railroads of Southeast Iowa

In 1900 a large crowd gathered in front of Union Depot to welcome William Jennings Bryan, Democratic candidate for President (he lost the 1900 election to William McKinley). In a typical day during the campaign Bryan gave four speeches, each one an hour long.

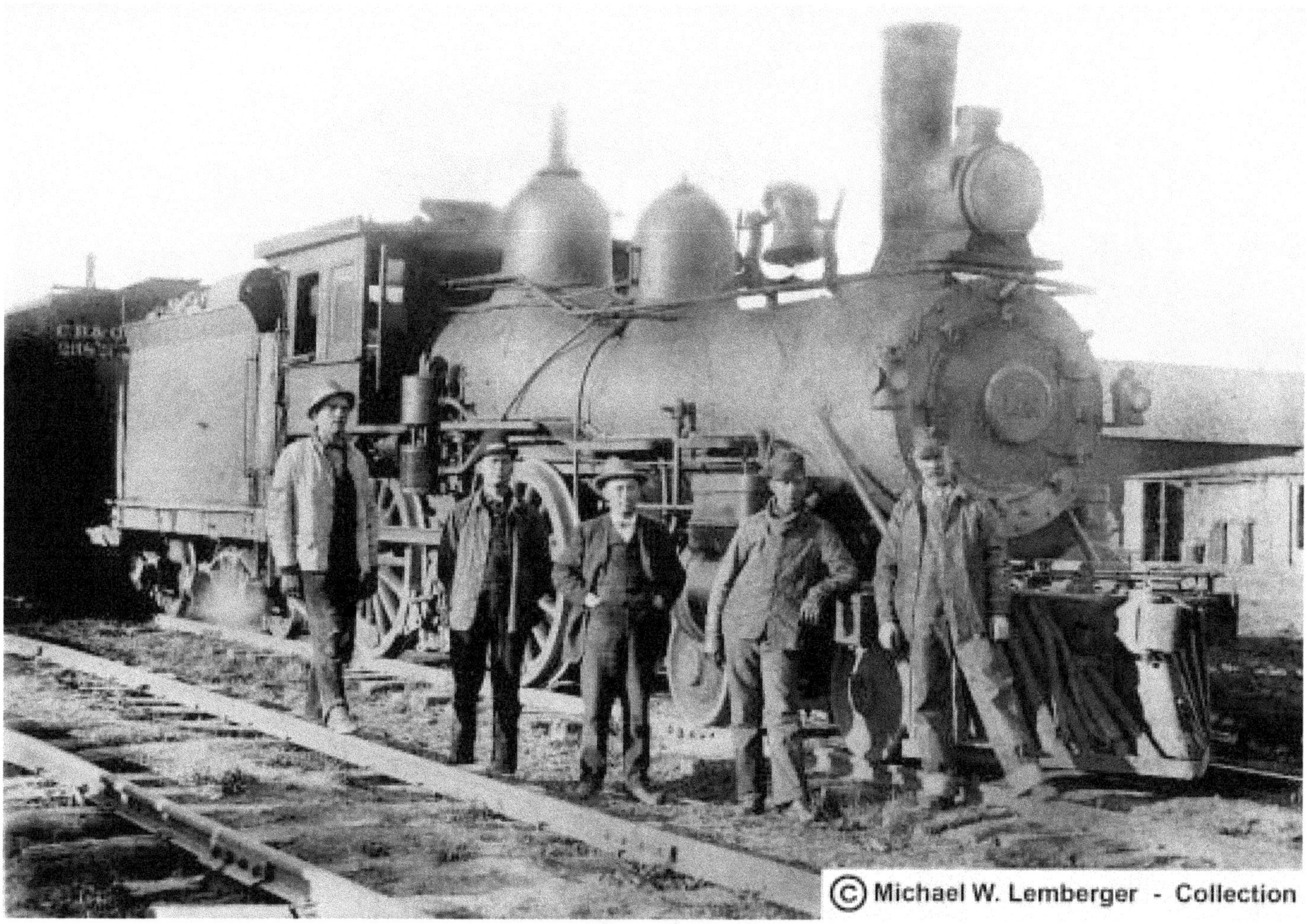
© Michael W. Lemberger - Collection

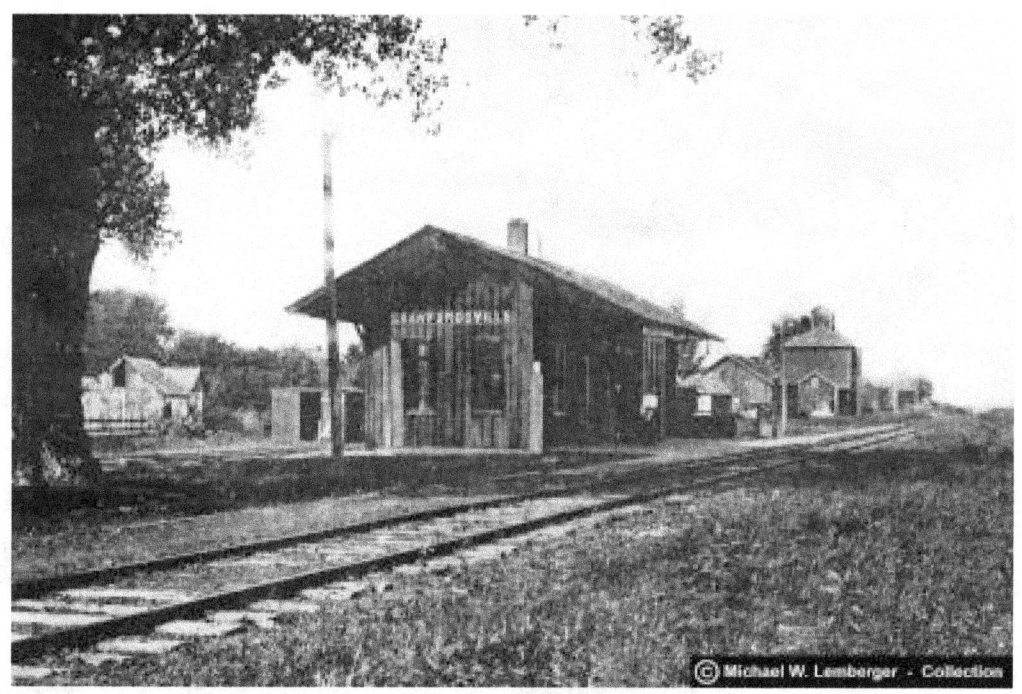

C.B. & Q. steam engine #118, with a crew, about 1900.

CRAWFORDSVILLE
© Michael W. Lemberger - Collection

C.B. & Q. depot at Crawfordsville, Iowa (Washington County) with grain elevator in the background.

Eldon, Iowa depot (Wapello County).

Milwaukee Road depot at Sherman Street, Ottumwa, looking toward the northeast.

**The Lemberger Collection**

C & N Railroad and Buxton, Iowa depot, looking east (Monroe County).

C. B. & Q. depot, Fairfield, Iowa (Jefferson County).

Postcard view of John Morrell & Company meatpacking plant on Iowa Avenue, looking south across the tracks toward the current site of the Cargill Meat Solutions plant.

# The Lemberger Collection

Note the sign on the building at right: East End Y.M.C.A.

1903 flood in Ottumwa, taken from the tower of Union Depot. Compare this view with a similar photo taken from the same location in 1900 (pages 32-33). At the north end of the Market Street bridge is a Milwaukee passenger train, probably en route to or from Cedar Rapids, pulled by a steam engine.

## The Lemberger Collection

The Race bridge is closest to the camera, with the Market Street bridge in the center and the Wabash bridge leading to Dain Manufacturing nearest the top of the photograph.

# Railroads of Southeast Iowa

1903 flood, Ottumwa. A west-bound steam engine plows through floodwater as it crosses Market Street and pulls into Union Depot. Steam engines could maneuver through as much as two feet of standing water without serious damage.

# The Lemberger Collection

1903 flood, Ottumwa, with the Union Depot at right. The train in front of the depot includes an unusual sight -- a caboose on the end of a passenger train.

1903 flood, Ottumwa. The Milwaukee bridge over the Race is to the left, with Union Depot to the right.

# The Lemberger Collection

# Railroads of Southeast Iowa

A crowd gathers at Union Depot, about 1910. Note the smokestack of the waterworks plant in the background. Blurs close to the camera show people moving during the long, slow exposure necessary to make this photograph. Notice the people standing on the roof above the building entrance. The Rock Island tracks are to the right of the depot. A water spigot used to refill tanks on the tenders is at lower left, arching over the track.

# The Lemberger Collection

Crowds frequently gathered at the depots to greet or see off celebrities or important groups. This scene is dated 1912. Note the horse-drawn luggage wagons and buggies, as well as the stack of milk cans at the center (near the base of the pole) and the people in the depot tower and looking out the windows.

Rock Island roundhouse, at Eldon, Iowa, photographed in 1909. The roundhouse, located north and west of the existing depot, contained 16 stalls used for engine repair. The building was torn down in the late 1940s.

Rock Island bridge over the Des Moines River at Eldon, photographed in 1911.

# The Lemberger Collection

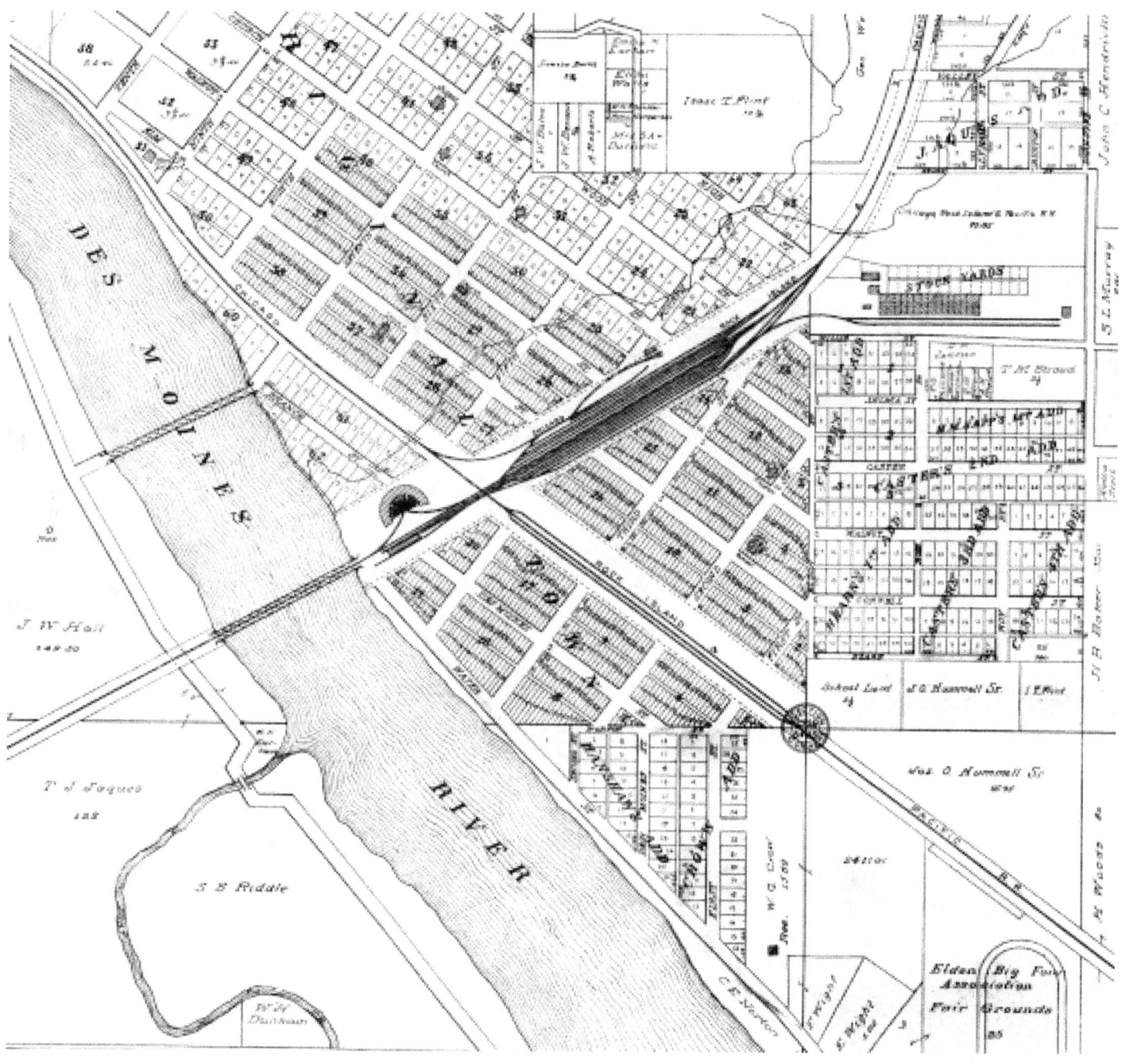

This 1908 map of Eldon, Iowa, shows the railroad yards and roundhouse at the heart of the town.

**Railroads of Southeast Iowa**

Steam engine # 1604 at the Blakesburg, Iowa Milwaukee Railroad depot in 1909. This is thought to be train #3. Its eastbound counterpart was train #8.

C.B. & Q. depot in Batavia, Iowa  March 24, 1917.

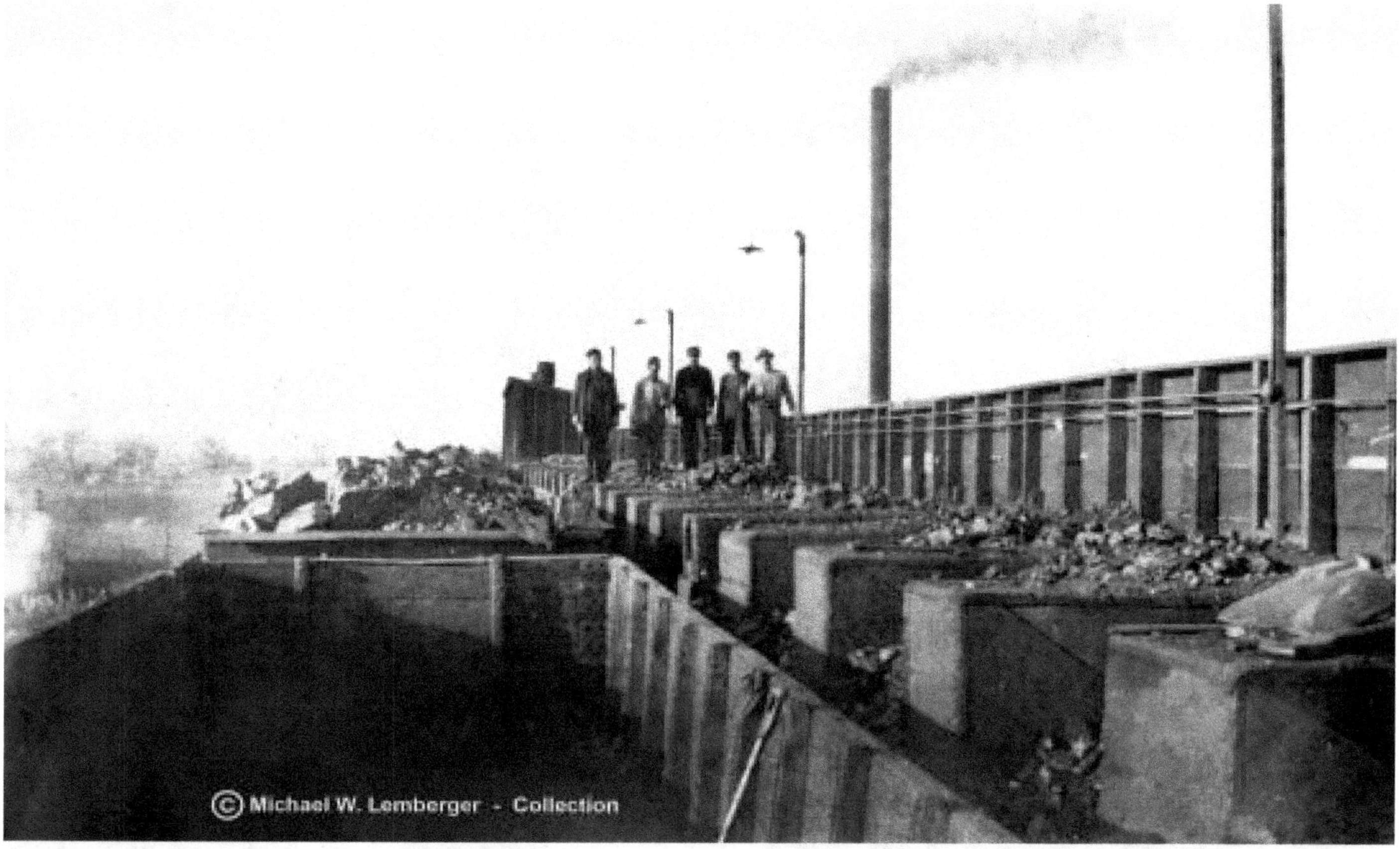
© Michael W. Lemberger - Collection

Crew atop hopper cars at Eldon, Iowa in 1912 are thought to be shoveling riprap.

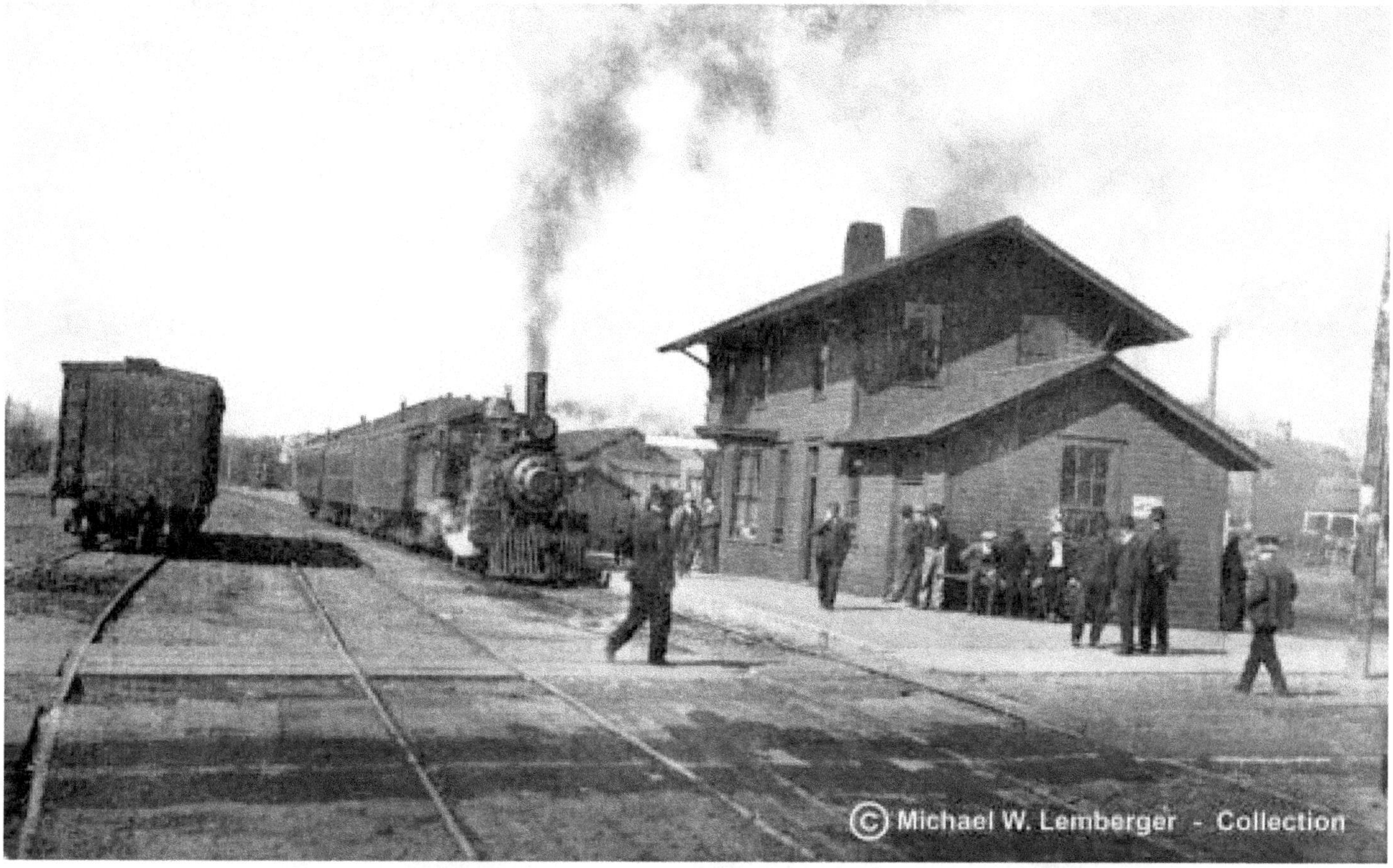
© Michael W. Lemberger - Collection

Steam locomotive at the Rock Island depot in What Cheer, Iowa (Keokuk County) in 1914.

Rock Island freight depot at 212 S. Union, Ottumwa. Street, Ottumwa, in 1911.

# The Lemberger Collection

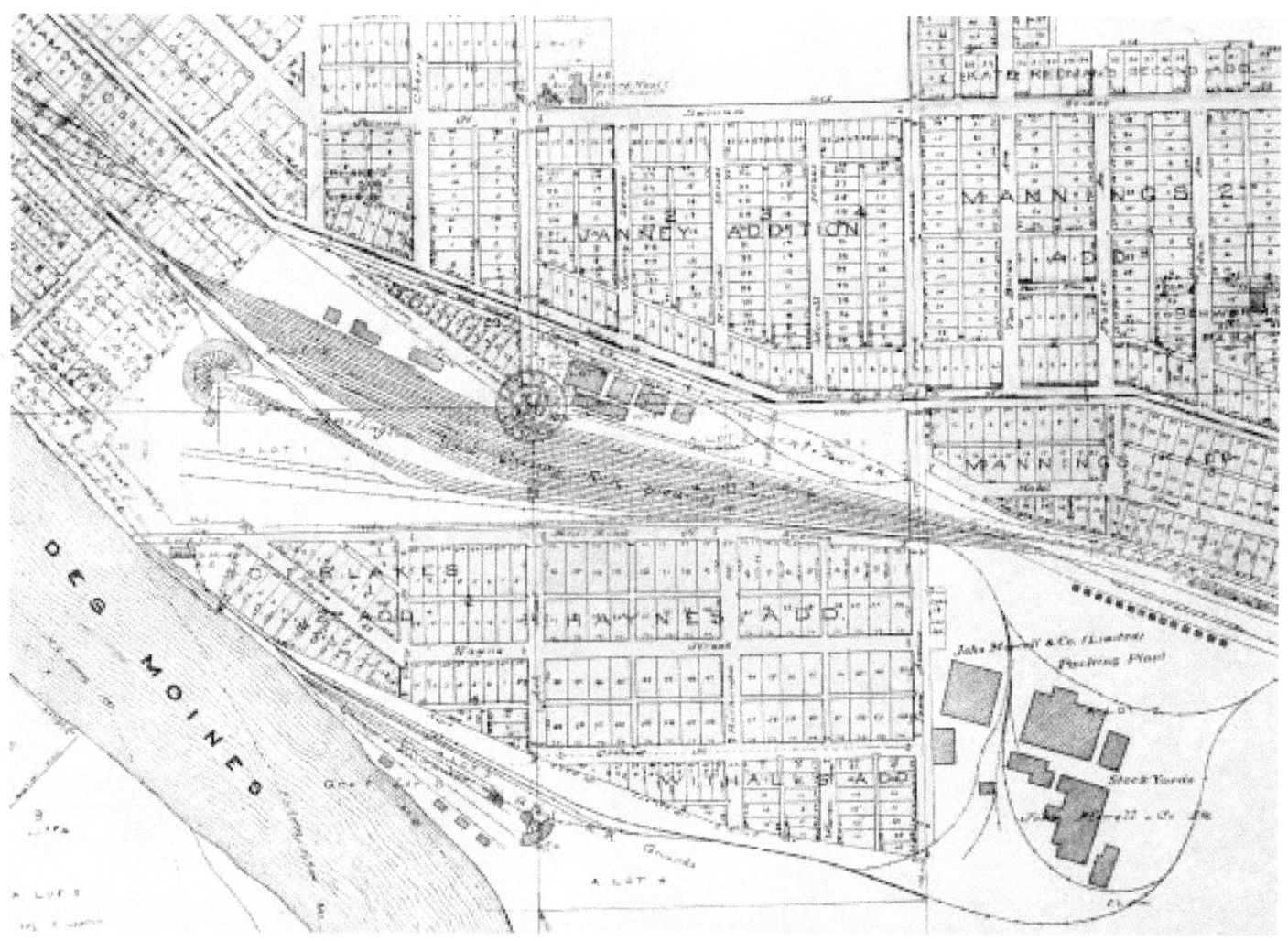

Rail yards in Ottumwa's east end in 1908. The C B & Q roundhouse is at center left, with the river running along the lower left corner. A Milwaukee roundhouse is at center bottom. John Morrell & Co. meatpacking plant is at lower right.

Office of the C.B. & Q. freighthouse, Ottumwa, in 1915.

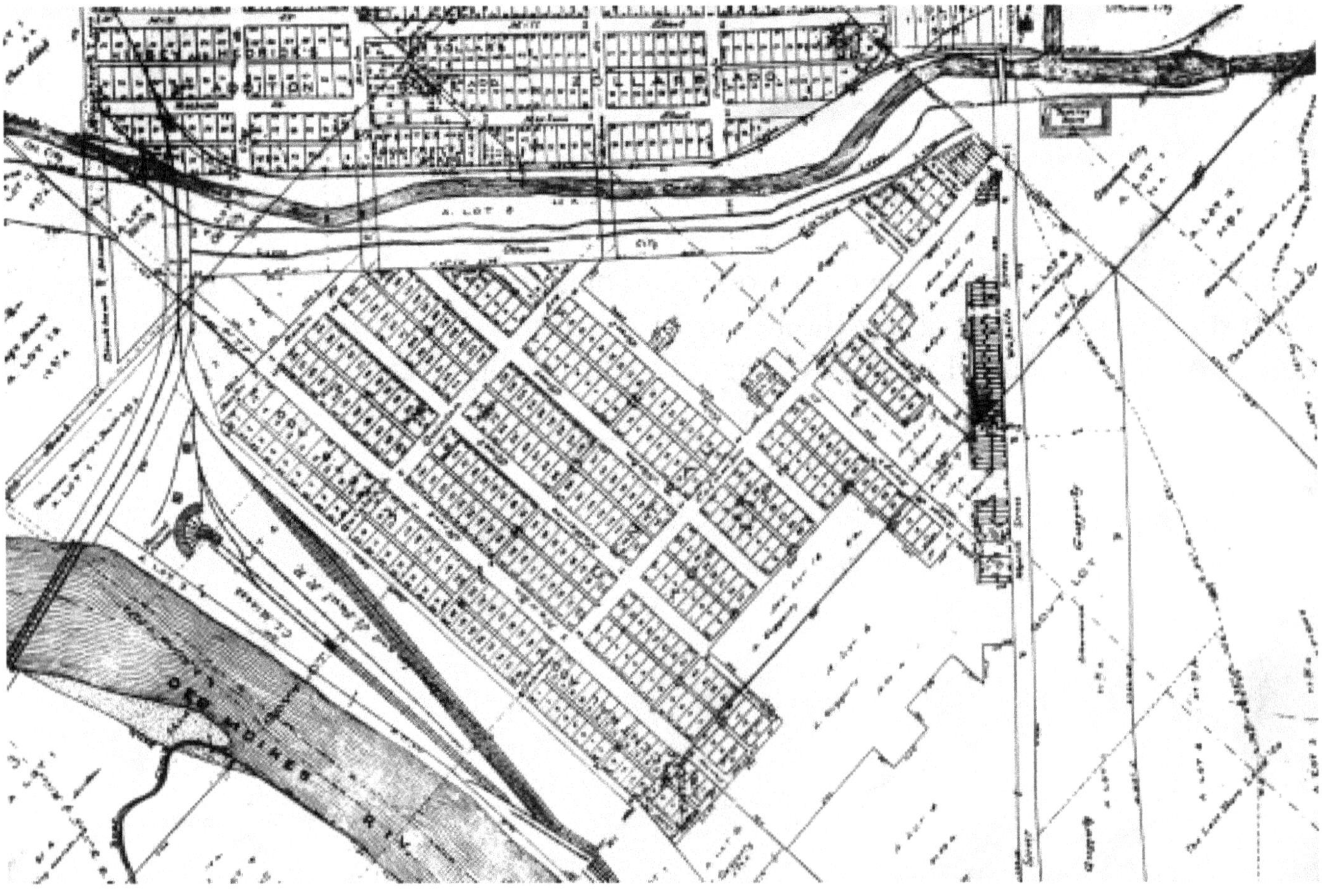

# The Lemberger Collection

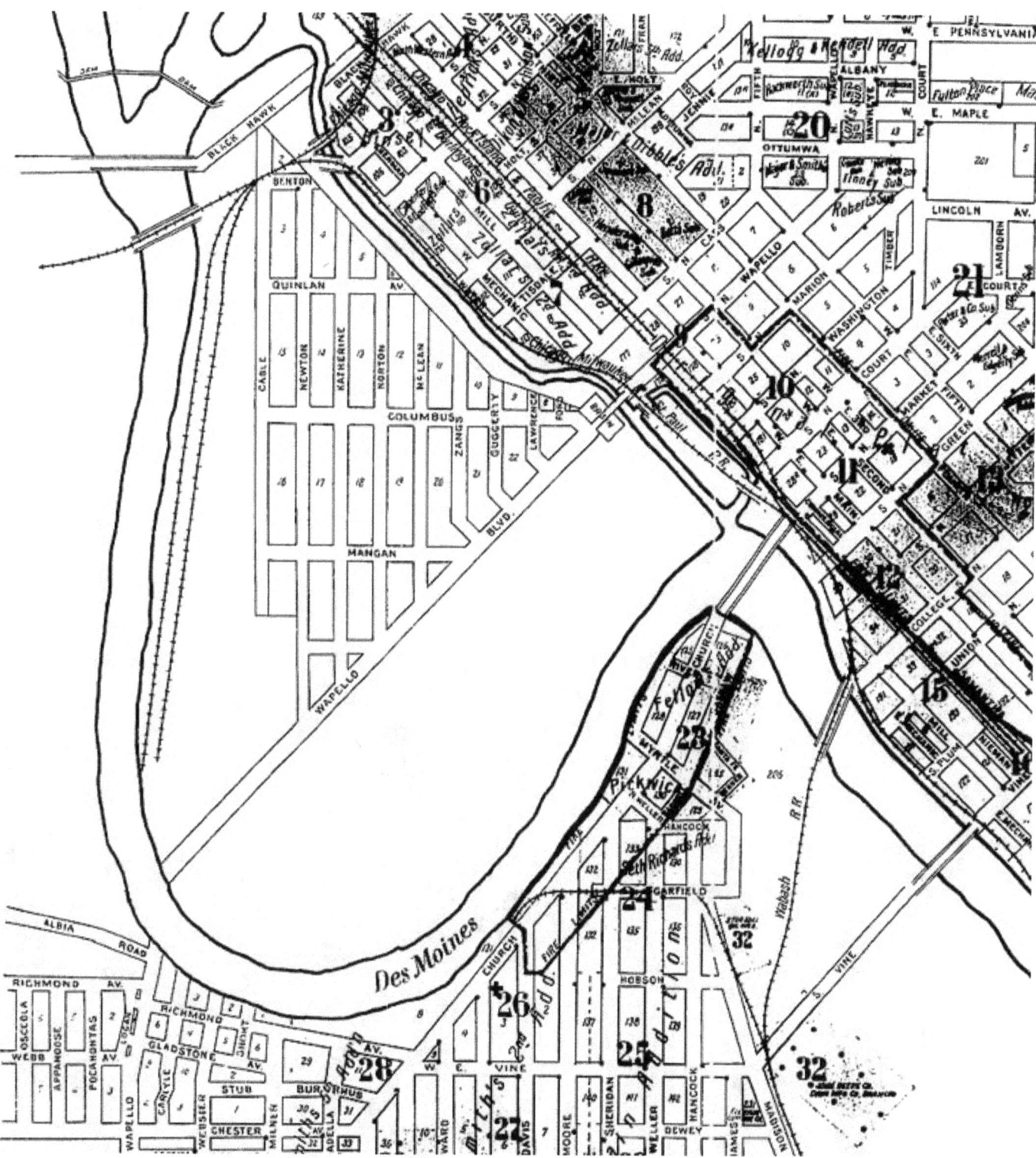

*(Above)* Map showing streets and railroads in Central Addition, 1917.
*(Left)* Map showing streets and railroads, including a roundhouse, in Central Addition, 1916. On this map, north is toward the top left corner.
Central Addition, platted in the 1890s, was promoted as the garden spot of Ottumwa, but repeated flooding led to the area being set aside as Ottumwa Park after the river-straightening project of the 1950s.

In 1934, the Burlington Route's Pioneer Zephyr made a record-time run from Denver to Chicago, passing through Ottumwa on its trip east. The next day, the train made a more leisurely journey back to Denver, stopping at major stations

# The Lemberger Collection

along the way. This photo was taken the day after the record run -- 1,000 miles non-stop, in just over 13 hours. The train is now on display at the Museum of Science and Industry in Chicago.

Burlington Route passenger bus and motor carrier, stopped on the northeast corner of North Green and Third, in Ottumwa, in 1931. The building directly behind the bus is the YMCA, then located at the corner of Green and Second.

# The Lemberger Collection

An array of teletypes and other communications equipment fill a railroad office and communications center, around 1940.

Steam locomotive #5355 went off the track in the late 1940s, but remained upright.

# The Lemberger Collection

The location of the wreck is not known.

Ottumwa roundhouse employees pose atop engine # 7227, on November 20, 1937.
This is most likely the day shift, including steamfitters, pipefitters, fire-knockers,
boilermakers, machinists and many other jobs.
The roundhouse operated around the clock with three full shifts of workers.
More than 300 men worked at the Milwaukee roundhouse
at its peak in the 1930s or 1940s.

# The Lemberger Collection

The Milwaukee Line suffered a derailment and fire on January 23, 1938.

In October 1937, former Presidential candidate and former Kansas Gov. Alf Landon came to Ottumwa. Crowds wait on the Jefferson Street viaduct. The Wabash depot is visible under the bridge, and the back of the Milwaukee freight house is at left.

# The Lemberger Collection

Governor Landon speaks from the back platform of his train. The tower of Union Depot is visible in the background. The Market Street bridge is to the left.

In May, 1939, the Milwaukee Railroad assembled what was said to be the world's largest extra gang. An extra gang was sent in to build or rebuild track when it was worn down or damaged beyond what a regular section gang could maintain.

# The Lemberger Collection

Derailment and wreck on the Rock Island line, November 13, 1938.

Milwaukee engine #493, Mikado 2-8-2 freight engine, photographed in December 1940.

# The Lemberger Collection

Steam engine #2057, probably a Rock Island or a C. B. & Q. engine, in the yards after the front of the locomotive was damaged. #2057 was a Prairie engine with a 2-6-2 configuration (two pony wheels, six drive wheels, two trailers).

A Milwaukee Railroad freight steam engine runs through snow-covered terrain between Blakesburg and Moravia, near the town of Foster, on February 13, 1937.

# The Lemberger Collection

# Railroads of Southeast Iowa

The Rock Island Railroad's Arizona Rocket used an Alco DL-107 locomotive to carry the Notre Dame football team through Eldon on December 13, 1940, after the team played a game in California,.

A Railway Express truck was damaged in an Ottumwa accident in 1937.

## The Lemberger Collection

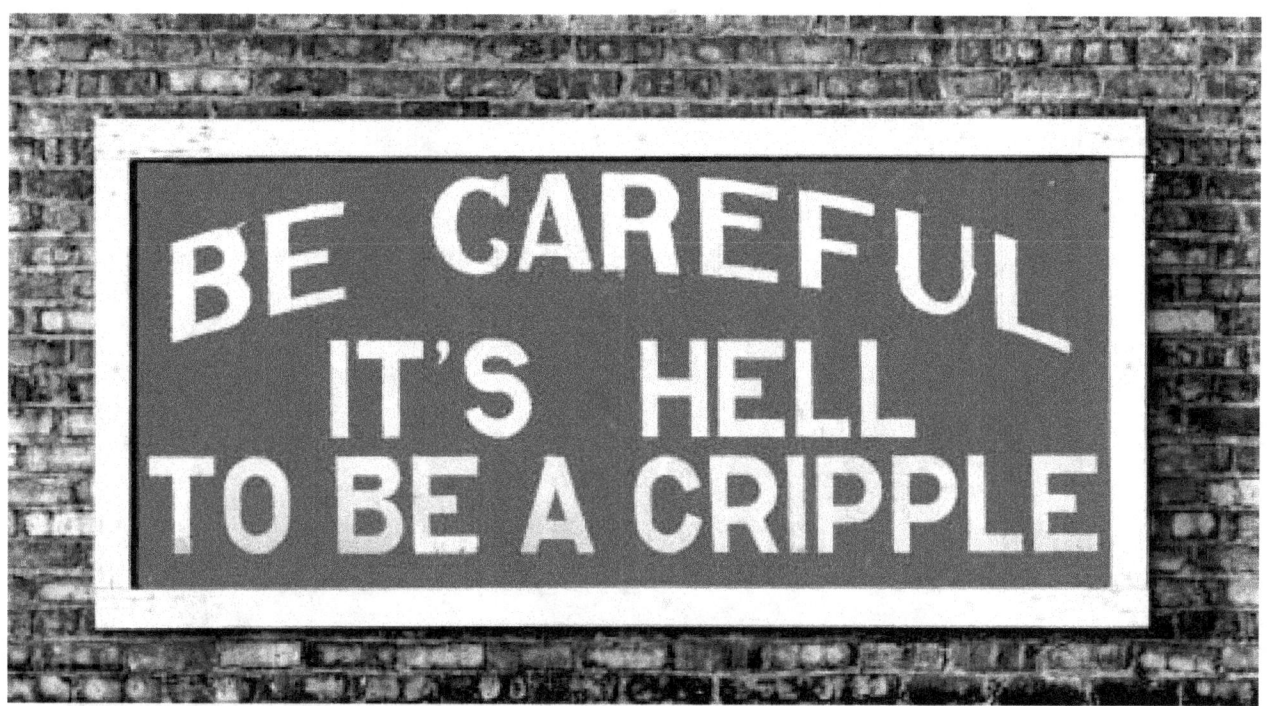

Long before OSHA, the Milwaukee Railroad encouraged workers to be cautious with a sign posted in the roundhouse -- December 1940.

Switching equipment and standard clock used at Union Depot in the 1940s and 1950s. Each employee was responsible for synchronizing his watch with the standard clock before every run.

Passengers disembark from the Silver Penthouse car of the C.B. & Q.'s California Zephyr using a roll-out platform, at Ottumwa's Union Depot. The hydro dam building is at left.

# The Lemberger Collection

Lounge car on a passenger train about 1945.

C.B. & Q. dining car, with a 3-D mural called "Branding Time" -- about 1945.

**The Lemberger Collection**

Burlington Railroad Vista Dome car -- July 1945.

# Railroads of Southeast Iowa

Steam locomotive, probably C.B. & Q., pulling a freight through southeastern Iowa in the 1940s. Most of the cars are stock cars and refrigerator cars. Stock cars were generally close to the engine, so the animals could be watered when the engine and tender were serviced. Refrigerator cars featured hopper doors on top where ice could be dropped in and chipped to keep goods frozen during shipping.

# The Lemberger Collection

Milwaukee Railroad coal chute and sand tower, with steam engine approaching -- 1940. Dry sand was sprayed under the wheels of the locomotive to add traction where needed.

# Railroads of Southeast Iowa

Aerial view of the C. B. & Q. railroad yards in Ottumwa's east end, near the Morrell meatpacking plant, in the 1940s. The street running across the bottom right corner of the photo is Iowa Avenue. Bridges visible on the river at left are Vine Street, railroad bridge to John Deere Ottumwa Works, Jefferson Street viaduct, and Market Street. Rock Island tracks are toward the right of the photo, and Milwaukee tracks are toward the river.

## The Lemberger Collection

In 1939, Davenport Locomotive Works, located in Davenport, Iowa, produced an industrial locomotive design with two traction motors and rod connections, rather than four motors. Seven units were produced through 1936. The Morrell locomotive is pictured at the Ottumwa meatpacking plant.

Presidential candidate Wendell Wilkie (bottom right) posed with the crew of his campaign train in Eldon, Iowa on September 17, 1940, just weeks before he was defeated as Franklin D. Roosevelt won his third term.

Derailment and fire of Mobilgas tank cars,
near Sigourney, Iowa - July 2, 1941.

# The Lemberger Collection

# Railroads of Southeast Iowa

Railroad office in Union Depot, 1940s.

Burlington Route semi near Wapello Street viaduct.

# The Lemberger Collection

The original GM FT diesel locomotives, in Ottumwa in the 1940s. GM loaned this four-engine combination (6,000 horsepower total) along with mechanics, in order to teach railroads how to use the new diesel technology.

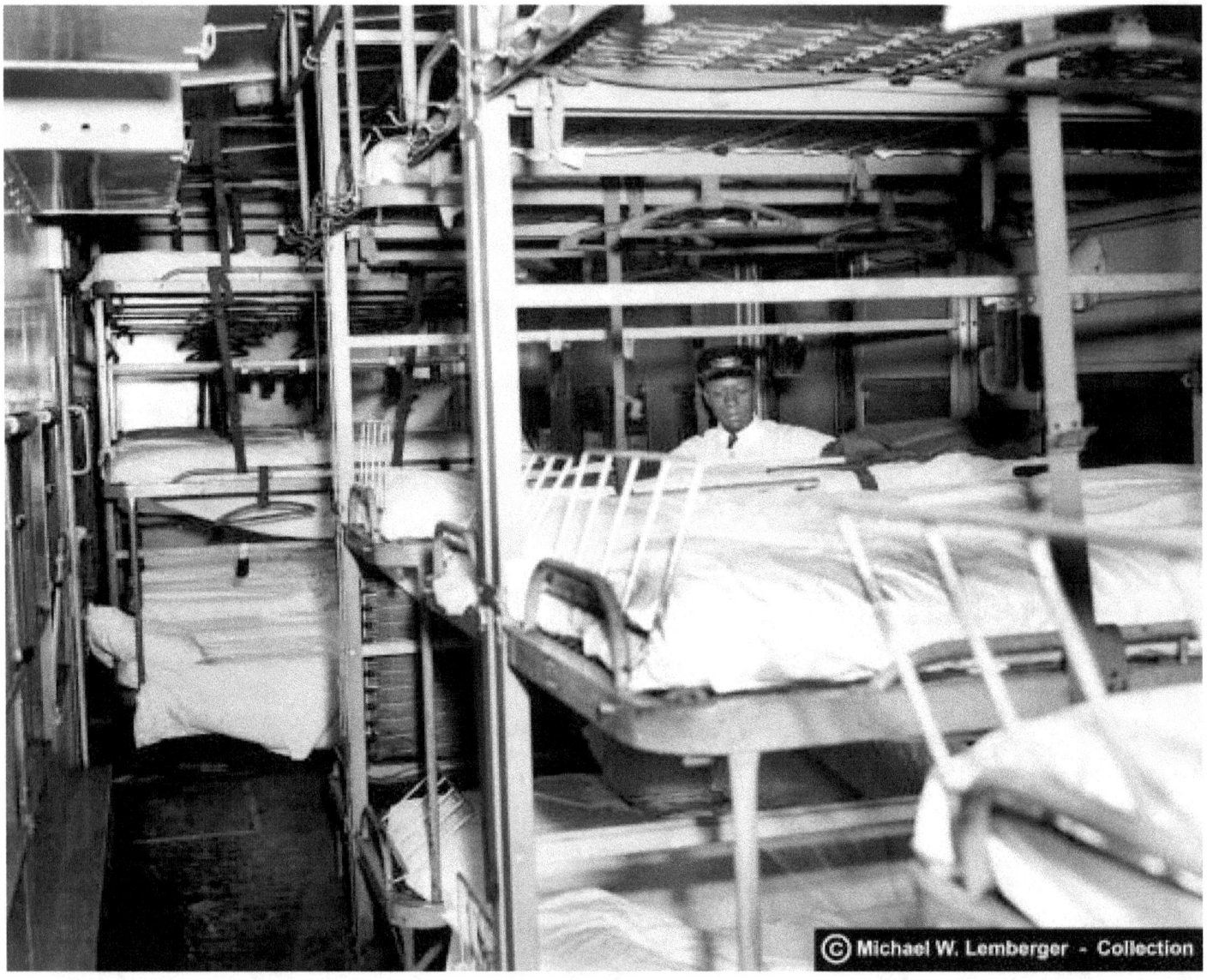

Economy-class Pullman cars. One car would be set aside for men, another for women. The man at center is a Pullman porter.

Certificate of Examination issued in 1942 to Edwin D. Lemberger, declaring him qualified to fill the position of conductor on the Chicago, Milwaukee, St. Paul and Pacific Railroad.

# The Lemberger Collection

Two C. B. & Q. steam engines on a snowy day in Ottumwa -- January 1940. The front engine is a Mikado 2-8-2 configuration. The back engine may be a more powerful locomotive known as a mountain engine.

Milwaukee Railroad yards near Wildwood Drive, Ottumwa, in a snowstorm.

# The Lemberger Collection

Doodlebug engine # 9813 in front of Union Depot in the 1940s. This type of engine carried the mail and small freight, had room for a few passengers, and sometimes pulled a passenger car. Doodlebug engines took the place of small or lightly-used regular trains.

Milwaukee Railroad yards off Wildwood Drive, Ottumwa -- 1940.

# The Lemberger Collection

The Milwaukee Railroad freight depot in Ottumwa, in 1942.
Jefferson Street Viaduct is visible in background.

During World War II, women went to work in many industries -- including the railroads. A crew of women are shown cleaning up a spill of feed or grain on the Burlington rails in April, 1943.

# The Lemberger Collection

Military troop transport sleeper cars on the Burlington Railroad, stopped in Ottumwa in September, 1944. Note the military policeman in naval uniform walking down the platform.

Railroad workers at the Ottumwa Naval Air Station, March 14, 1943.

West leg of the Milwaukee Wye Bridge and Sherman Street depot in 1945. This side of the depot was seldom photographed.

# The Lemberger Collection

Milwaukee Restaurant, 1019 Sherman, near the Milwaukee Railroad's Sherman Street depot. In 1943, the restaurant was operated by Mrs. Lucille Fox. Milwaukee Road crews rented rooms upstairs which they used on layovers. The area is now part of Marina Gateway.

Milwaukee Railroad derailment, about 1946.

Milwaukee Railroad -- wooden bridge at Harrow's Branch, Ottumwa, with helper units at rear of train.

# The Lemberger Collection

Employees of the Railway Express Agency pose with one of the express trucks, April 1946.

Souvenir ribbon from the Miami Beach convention of the Brotherhood of Railroad Trainmen, September 1950.

Milwaukee Railroad train in the Race channel of the Des Moines River after a derailment in April 1947, on the west leg of the Wye bridge. Switch engine #1551 went into the race, and the crew members -- engineer Curt Adcock, fireman Bill Wells, conductor Red Chambers, switchman Cleave Carnahan, and switchman Terry Owens -- ended up in the water. All survived.
Engineer Adcock was dragged to the bottom of the race when his raincoat caught between the engine and the tender.
Fireman Wells, who was unable to swim, seized a tree trunk which kept him afloat until he was rescued. He then went home, changed clothes, and returned to work.
The bridge, which was being used mainly as a turnaround for locomotives and trains at the time, was not rebuilt after this accident.

# The Lemberger Collection

A crane pulls Engine #1551
out of the river...

... and sets it
upright once more.

*(Above and right, top and bottom)* Aftermath of a fire in the Rock Island roundhouse in Eldon, on January 5, 1948.
*(Right, top)* Alco RS-1 engine seen through the hole in the wall.
*(Right, bottom)* Small doodlebug engine after the fire.

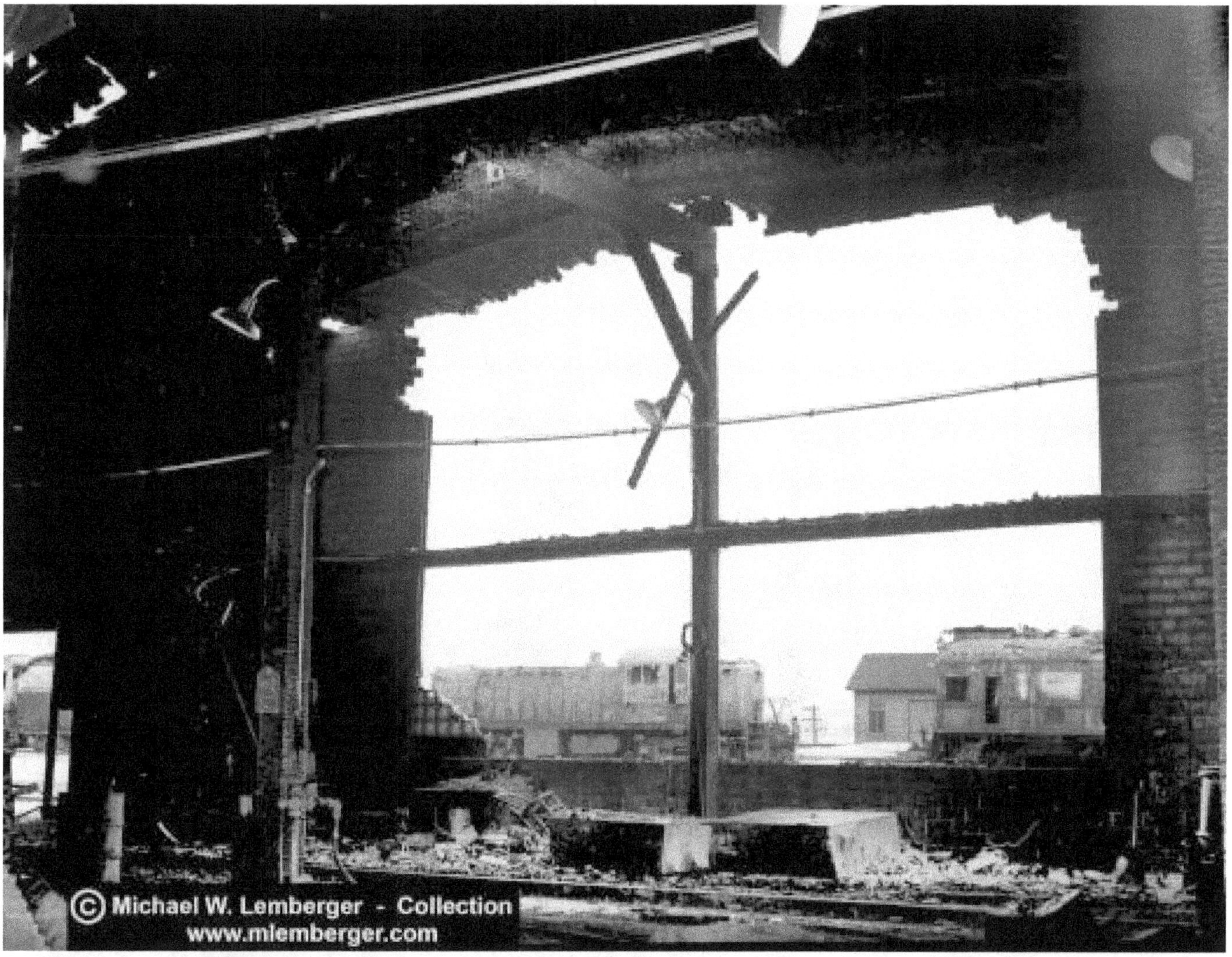

# The Lemberger Collection

# Railroads of Southeast Iowa

# The Lemberger Collection

*(Above)* September 9, 1948 railroad wreck and fire.

*(Left)* Milwaukee Railroad derailment and burned bridge, September 9, 1948.

Steam locomotive and freight train, between Ottumwa and Agency, Iowa.

# The Lemberger Collection

Aerial view of the Milwaukee Railroad yards and roundhouse west of Ottumwa, looking east toward the downtown area. The street at bottom right is Wildwood Drive. Highway 34 now runs parallel to the tracks, approximately from the bottom right to the top right corner.

Identification card issued by the Miama Beach, Florida, police department to delegates to the national convention of the Brotherhood of Railroad Trainmen, held in Miami Beach in 1950.

*(Above)* The crowd awaits former President Harry S Truman *(right)*, when he visited Ottumwa in May, 1950.

# The Lemberger Collection

Rock Island Railroad wreck near Belknap, Iowa -- 1950.

Burlington Railroad E-7 A & B diesel passenger engines in Ottumwa -- 1950s.
*A* models included a crew cab while *B* models did not.

Union Depot before start of remodeling -- February, 1950. The tower peak had been removed earlier.

The remaining tower section was removed in May, 1950.

## The Lemberger Collection

Remodeling well under way -- August, 1950.

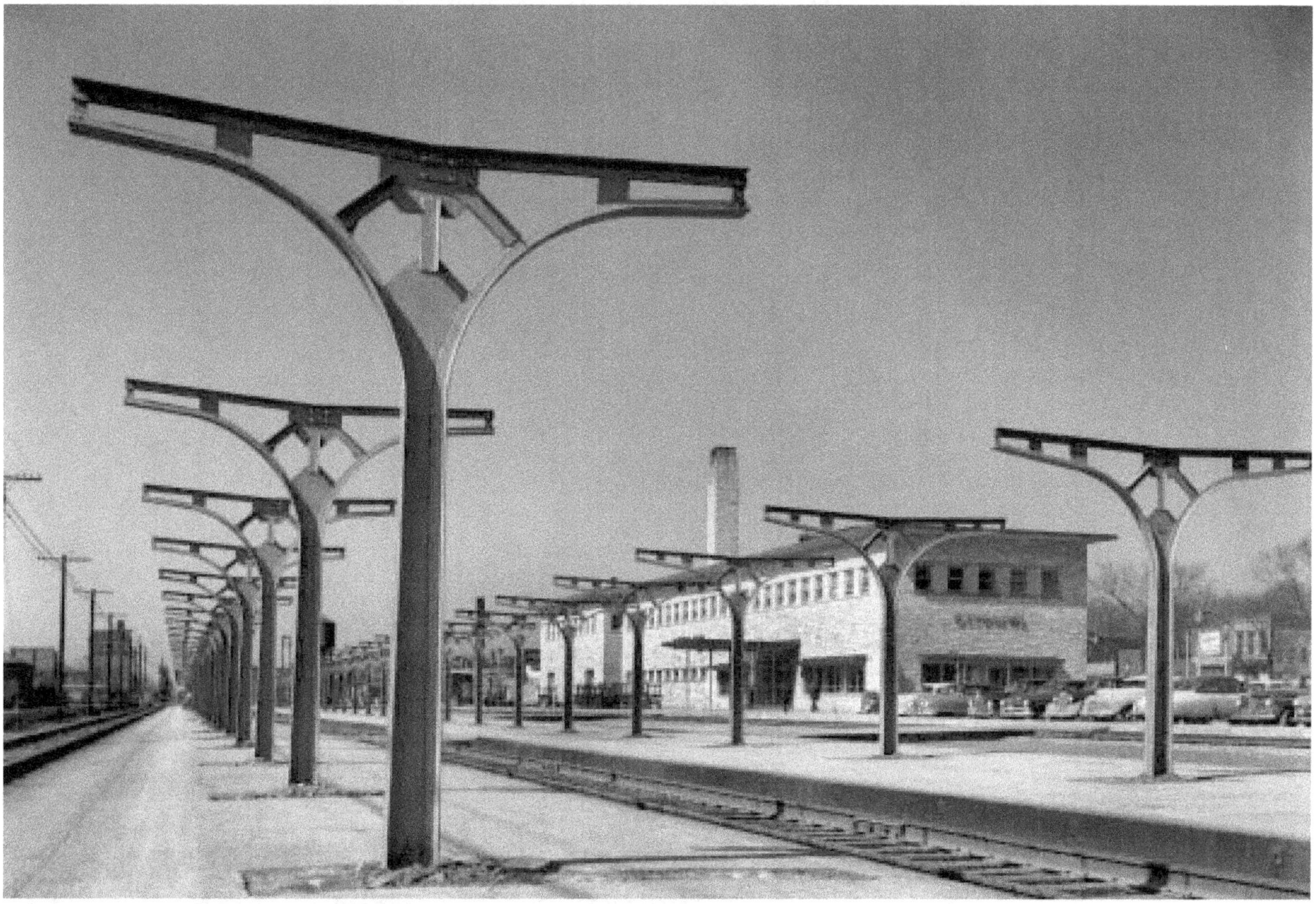

Steel frames were put in place to support shelters for passengers as they embarked and disembarked.

Completed depot from the track side -- 1951.

Completed depot and Ballingall Park from Main Street -- 1951.

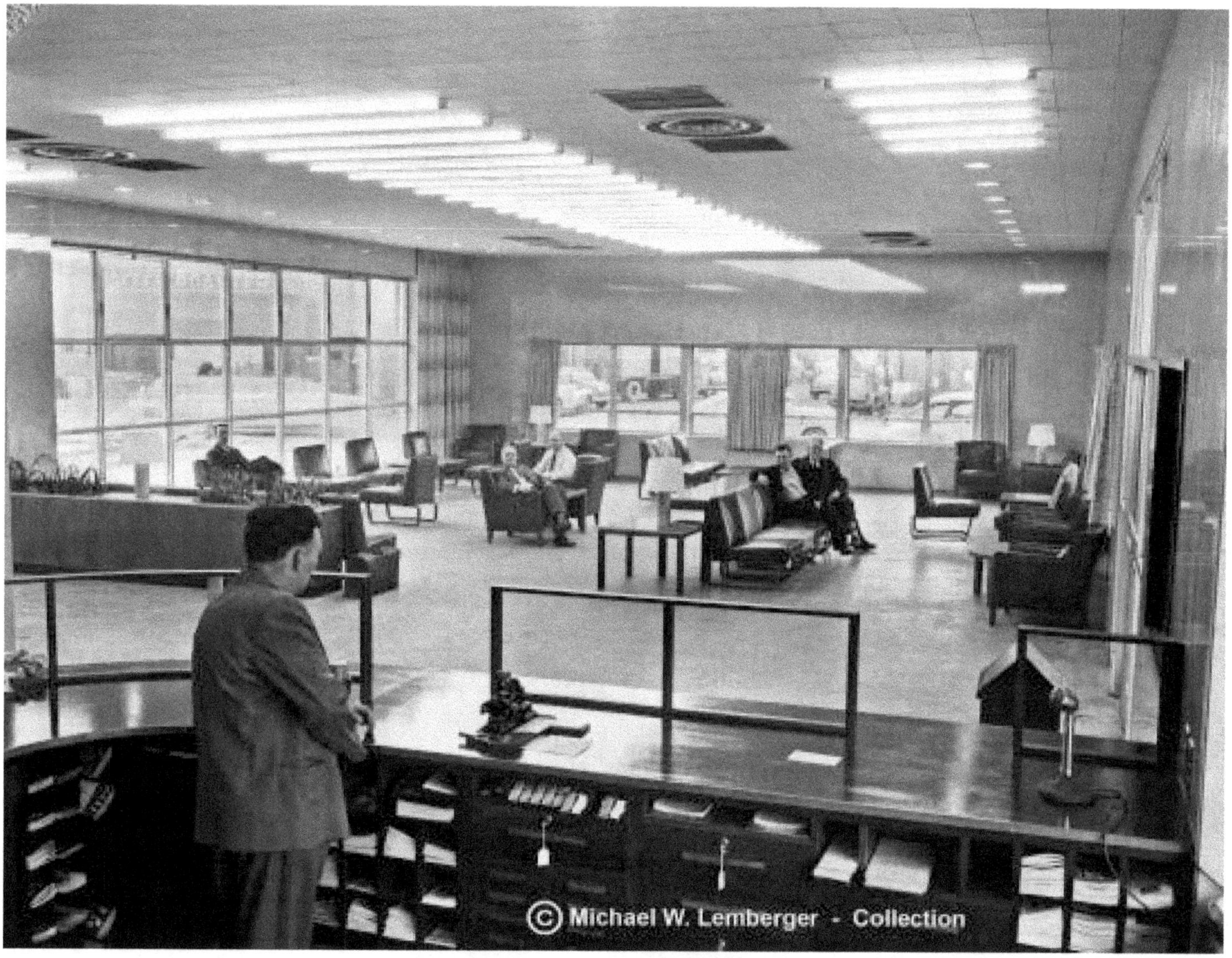
© Michael W. Lemberger - Collection

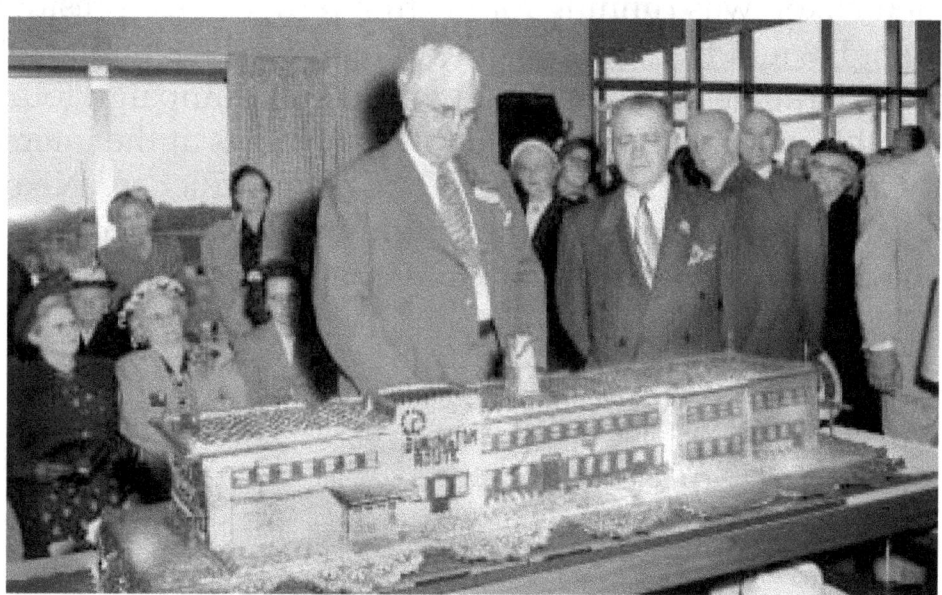

Waiting room -- 1951.

Grand opening of the newly-remodeled depot, complete with cake cutting.

Richard and Pat Nixon, campaigning from the back of a train. The photo, taken in 1952 when Nixon was running for his first term as vice-president under President Dwight D. Eisenhower, is thought to be a public relations opportunity rather than an actual whistle-stop campaign tour. Richard and Pat Nixon lived at the Tisdale Apartments at the intersection of Fourth and Green in Ottumwa during World War II. Richard Nixon was a U.S. Navy officer stationed at the Ottumwa Naval Air Station, and Pat Nixon worked at Union Bank as a teller.

# The Lemberger Collection

An eastbound Burlington Route passenger train crossing Market Street in the late 1950s. The remodeled depot is at center right.

Rock Island Railroad Cliffland Depot (Wapello County), taken in the 1950s.

Looking eastward from the Jefferson Street viaduct in the late 1950s.
East Main street runs along the top left corner of the photograph.
The "passenger" train at left (on track Main #1) is an express made up of mail express cars with a single passenger coach at the rear, allowing the train
to operate under passenger train regulations even though
it might be carrying no passengers at all.
The freight train at right (on track Main #2) is an early
intermodel "piggyback" train, with each car carrying just one semitrailer.
Later freight cars were built long enough for each car to carry two semitrailers.

# The Lemberger Collection

Aerial view of the Milwaukee Railroad roundhouse in the yards near Wildwood Drive on a snowy day, showing the turntable at center and the roundhouse at lower left. At its peak, the roundhouse operated around the clock, with more than 300 workers employed in repairing and maintaining locomotives.

Milwaukee Railroad bridge across the race. It is believed that the workmen pictured here are in the process of taking out the bridge, as part of the river-straightening project.

# The Lemberger Collection

Burlington Route freight speeding under a trestle bridge between Ottumwa and Agency.
Note the truss rod span supporting the center of the bridge.

Burlington Route Engine #4000, one of the first locomotives to be given a "streamlined" makeover, was originally C. B. & Q. engine #3002. The sheeting covers a steam locomotive which is a sister engine to the one now

displayed at the Ottumwa depot (see next page). Named the "Aeolus" (God of the winds, in Greek mythology), she was called "Big Alice , the Goon" (from a Popeye cartoon) by her crews. The locomotive is now on display in La Crosse, WI.

Burlington Engine #3001, while still in service and en route to Ottumwa. This engine was given to the city in 1959 and displayed at the Ottumwa depot.

1955 postcard showing the Burlington Route's Nebraska Zephyr.

# The Lemberger Collection

Dedication and unveiling of Burlington Engine #3001, outside the Ottumwa Depot in 1959. George M. Foster (at podium) was instrumental in obtaining the engine and moving it to its permanent display position between Ballingall Park and the depot. Members of the Foster family later contributed funds to renovate the engine after years of weather had taken a toll.

The locomotive is known as a Pacific because of the 4-6-4 configuration of wheels -- four pony wheels, six drive wheels, and four trailing wheels.

C.B. & Q. engine #5632, taken in October 1956 in Ottumwa.
Note the fold-up coupler on the front of the locomotive, common at the time on many passenger locomotives.

# The Lemberger Collection

C.B. & Q. Detector Car #3, taken in July 1959. Detector cars were used to inspect track, finding split or broken rails.

Diamond stack engine #35 in Ottumwa in 1959, as it toured the country with the mail-sorting car which was the first one used in the country.

In 1959, the Burlington Railroad's Pioneer Zephyr made its last run east, en route to the Museum of Science and Industry in Chicago where it remains on display today.

# The Lemberger Collection

The Pioneer Zephyr on its last run through Ottumwa in 1959, as it pulled away from the Ottumwa Depot and headed for Market Street crossing.

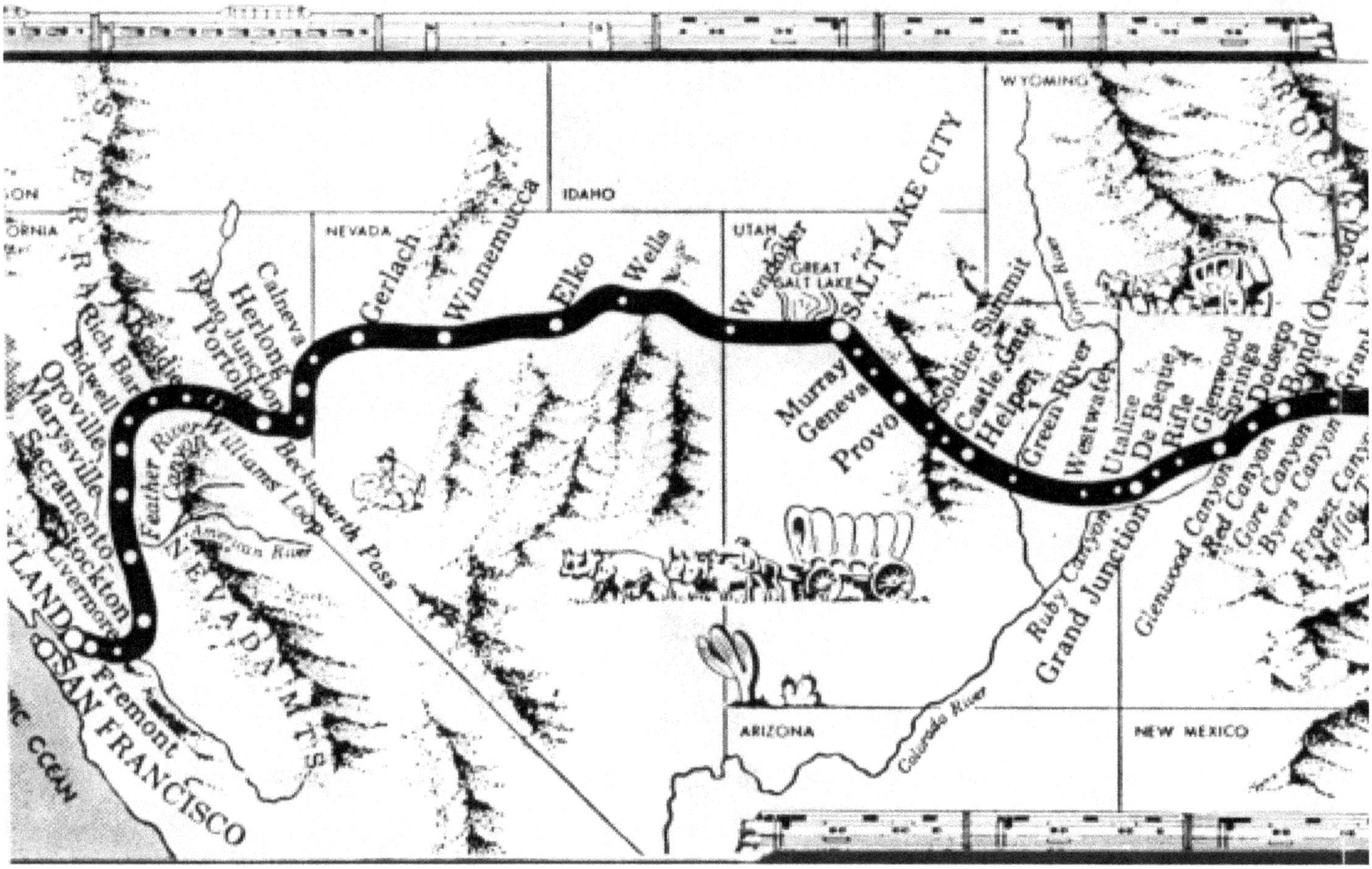

1958 route map of the California Zephyr passenger trains, showing each station stop along the route.

Thirty-year membership card of the Brotherhood of Railroad Trainmen.

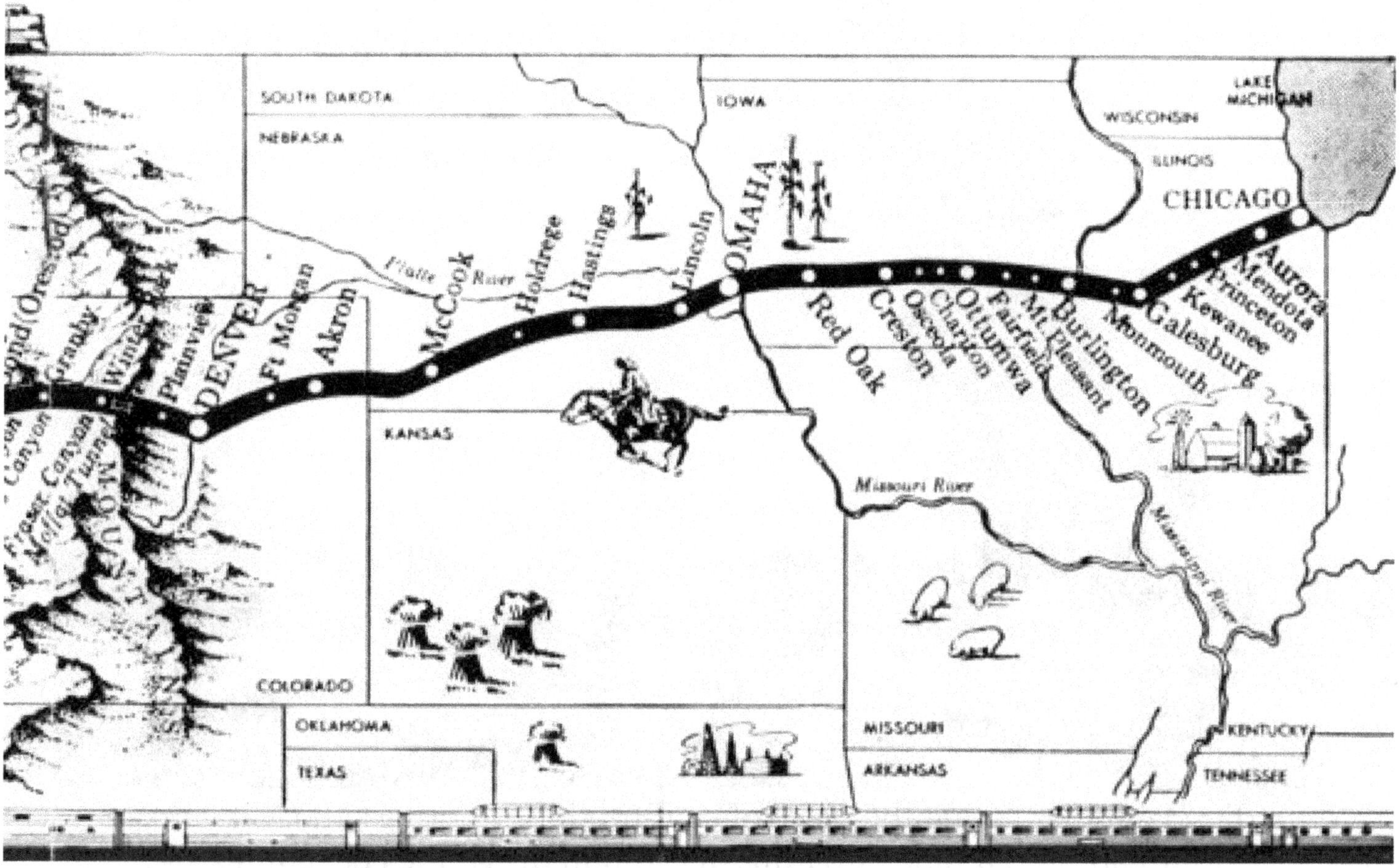

# The Lemberger Collection

Record book used by train crews to record their trips and time worked. This book, provided by the railroad unions, is from 1959.

# Railroads of Southeast Iowa

With diesel engines taking the place of coal-fired locomotives, the Milwaukee Railroad used a Buick Roadmaster to pull down the coal chute at the yards west of Ottumwa.

Coal dust billows as the chute falls -- April 1, 1958.

## The Lemberger Collection

In September 1960, a passenger train pulled by Illinois Central Railroad steam locomotive # 790 made two round trips between Ottumwa and Cedar Rapids. The engineer was Charlie ("Chewing Gum") Gould. The last steam excursion train going over the Milwaukee tracks, this train ran on a Sunday morning.
The two white flags on the front of the locomotive show that it was an "extra" train. Hedrick School is visible at center on the horizon.

Cleanup begins after a Rock Island Railroad derailment two miles east of Centerville on October 30, 1966. Eleven cars went off the track.

# The Lemberger Collection

Repairing the overhead pedestrian walkway across the tracks at Iowa Avenue near the Morrell meatpacking plant -- January 1963.

Rock Island Railroad derailment one mile north of Drakesville, at the Belknap siding, on November 20, 1969. Seventeen cars went off the rails.

# The Lemberger Collection

C.B. & Q. coal chute, photographed in April 1963.
The round cylinder at the top of the front corner is a sand tank,
allowing locomotives to be resupplied with coal and sand in just one stop.

The C. B. & Q.'s California Zephyr approaches Iowa Avenue from the west, leaving Ottumwa on an east-bound run to Chicago -- March 2, 1970.

# The Lemberger Collection

The California Zephyr leaves Ottumwa behind, passing under the Highway 34 bridge -- March 2, 1970.

Burlington Engine # 35 pulls the first car built for the sole purpose of sorting mail while en route between cities, while on a 1970 visit to Ottumwa. (The engine and mail car are also pictured on page 125, on an earlier visit.)
The first railway post office was operated on the Hannibal & St. Joseph Railroad, later a part of the Burlington Lines. The car was built at Hannibal, Missouri.

*(Right, above)* Interior of the mail car.

*(Right, below)* Sorting boxes used on the route between Chicago and Denver.

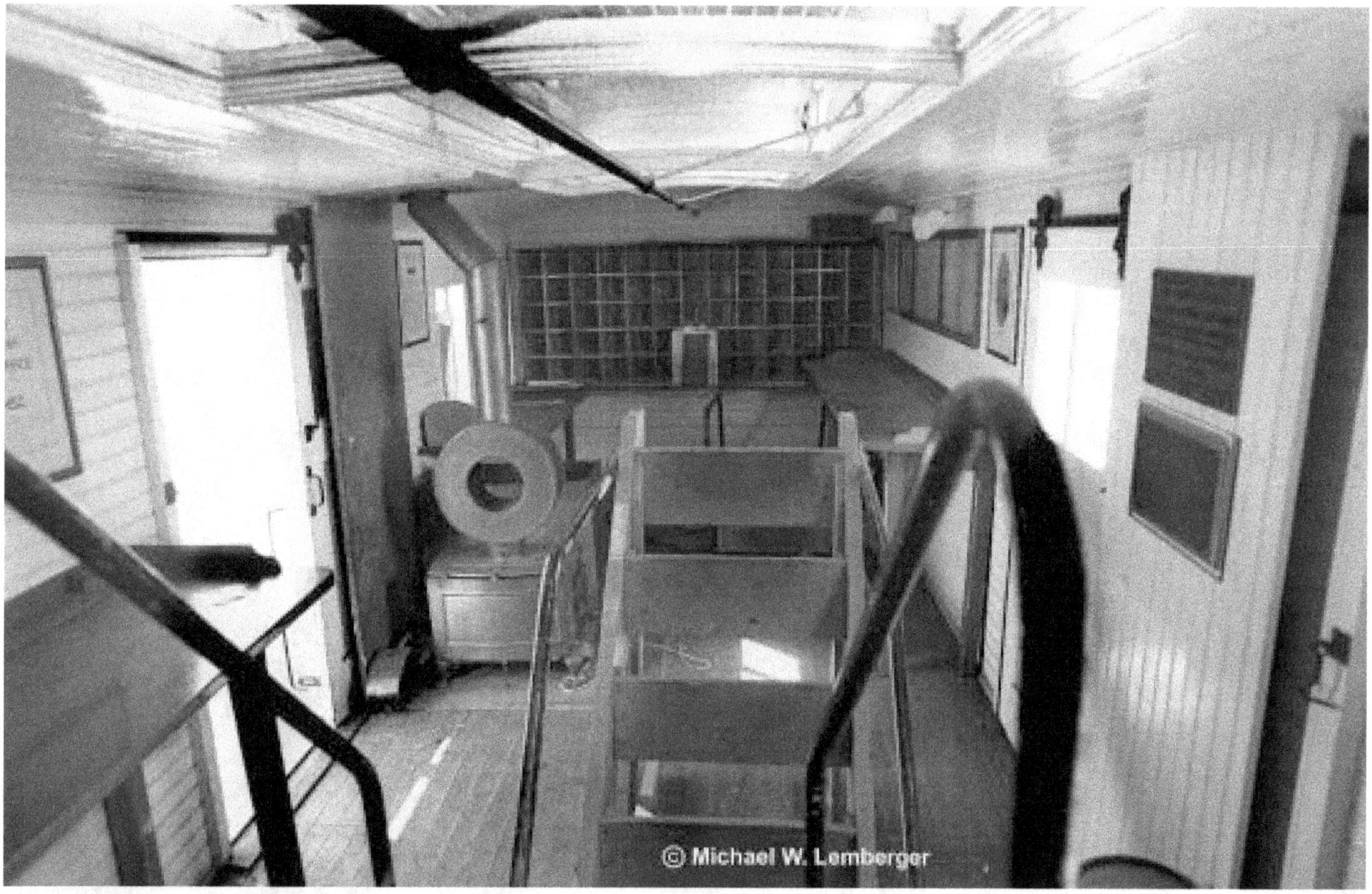
© Michael W. Lemberger

DENVER
BIG THOMPSON
FORT BRIDGER
BEAR RIVER
ECHO CANON
STILLWATER
© Michael W. Lemberger

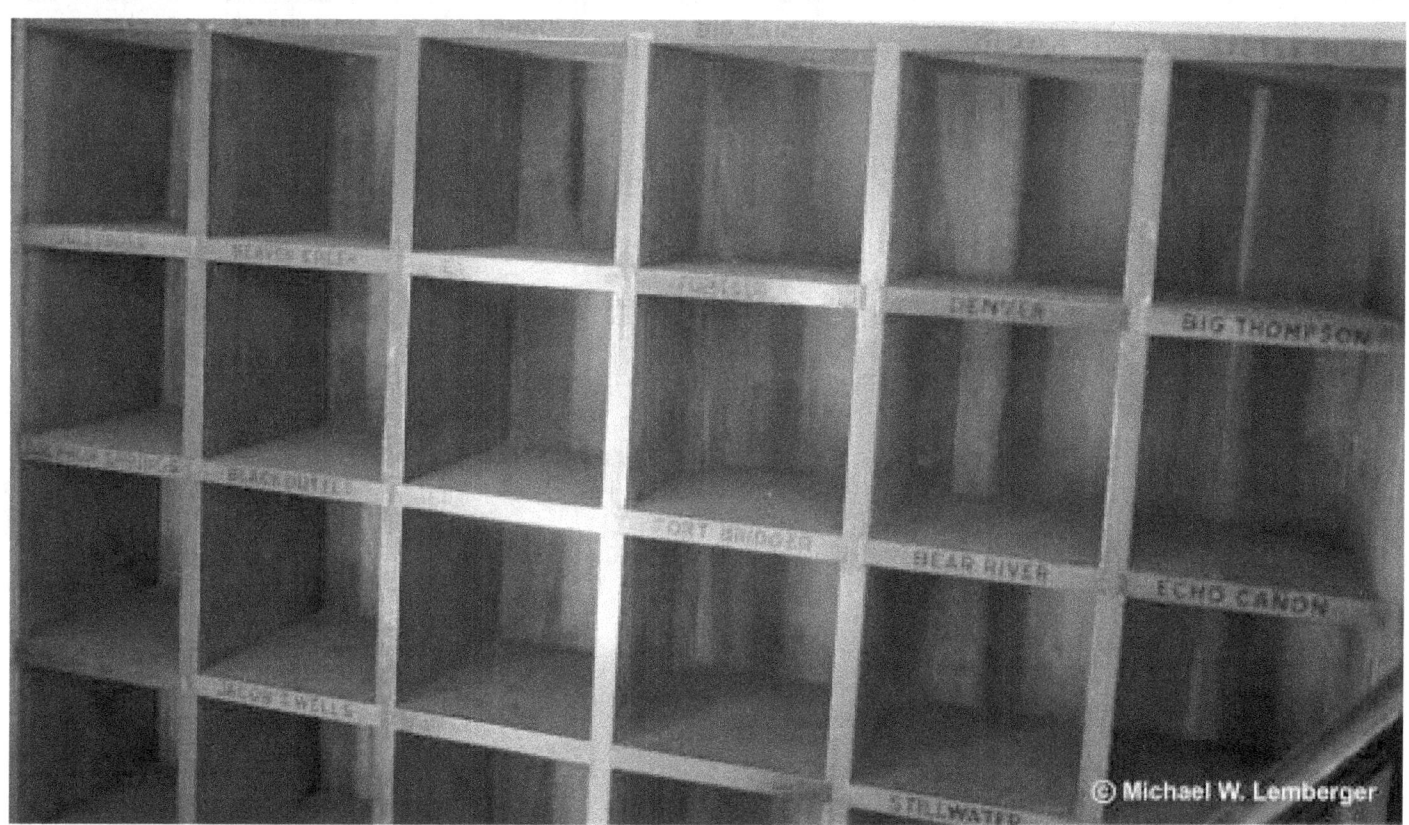

Railroad detective Dick Campbell inspects the aftermath of a derailment of a Burlington Northern freight at Four Mile Bridge west of Ottumwa -- September 10, 1970. The structure of the bridge is barely visible beyond the derailed cars.

# The Lemberger Collection

Tracks at sunset, Eldon, Iowa -- December 1970. The depot is at right.

# Railroads of Southeast Iowa

# The Lemberger Collection

The derailment of a load of live munitions on the Burlington Northern led to a explosion and fire. The wreck occurred west of Ottumwa
near Dudley on August 17, 1971.
Brakeman Bill Peters ran into the fire to uncouple cars that were not involved so the engine could pull them out.

The rail bridge on the Norfolk & Western line, over the Des Moines River just downstream from Market Street in Ottumwa, after it collapsed July 16, 1973 as the result of a derailment. A chain on a John Deere flat car caught on the bridge structure. The bridge ran from downtown to the John Deere Ottumwa Works.

In December 1974, workers from American Bridge & Steel laid in a steel girder span to replace the span which collapsed in July 1973. The replacement span was taken from an abandoned Burlington Northern line in Missouri.
The bridge later went out of service and became part of a walking trail.

Crossing the tracks in Eldon in a snowstorm -- March 25, 1975.

# Railroads of Southeast Iowa

Milwaukee Railroad derailment directly under Highway 63 near Memorial Lawn Cemetery -- July 16, 1973.

# The Lemberger Collection

Welding rails in Ottumwa -- November 1973.

A Milwaukee Railroad derailment on October 17, 1973 left James Gee's yard at 220 Kenyon Avenue a mess. This photograph was a time exposure (note the star trails in the sky).

# The Lemberger Collection

The photographer used a technique called painting with flash, locking the camera
locked in position while he walked around the scene with a flash unit.
The exposure time was about three minutes.

Eldon Y, looking west (before the overpass was built on Highway 16).

Trains often blocked the Market Street crossing in Ottumwa -- here, in March 1975.

# The Lemberger Collection

The Wabash depot at Moravia, Iowa (Appanoose County) taken in 1975.

Crew change on a Rock Island train near the Eldon depot -- March 25, 1975.

# The Lemberger Collection

Eldon, Iowa depot (Wapello County), taken in 1975.

Two boys run across the tracks ahead of a Burlington Northern train,

# The Lemberger Collection

Batavia, Iowa, June 24, 1975.

The Freedom Train made a 45-minute stop in Ottumwa, July 1, 1975. The steam engine stopped mainly to pick up water.

Milwaukee Railroad derailment on the bridge approach just east of Quincy Avenue in Ottumwa -- June 1975.

# The Lemberger Collection

Explorer Scouts from Post # 30 cleaned a Burlington Northern GP 20 diesel locomotive and caboose on display at the 1975 Oktoberfest celebration.

A Burlington Northern coal train derailed Oct. 20, 1975 five miles west of Fairfield, sending 19 cars off the tracks.

# The Lemberger Collection

The accident happened near Barnhart Station. A defective roller bearing was thought to be the cause. The derailed cars contained nearly 2,000 tons of coal.

Crews used side boom cats brought in from Galesburg, Illinois, to clean up a coal

# The Lemberger Collection

train derailment on the Burlington Northern west of Fairfield on October 20, 1975.

City and Burlington Northern officials hoisted flags on a new flagpole in Ballingall Park (near the depot) on October 17, 1975.

# The Lemberger Collection

Empty cars of a 100-car Burlington Northern coal train headed west near the Ottumwa depot. The passenger canopy is at left and Market Street is near the top.

The derailment of a Burlingon Northern safety check car injured seven workers just east of the South Main Street overpass in Albia, Iowa

# The Lemberger Collection

(Monroe County) on May 31, 1977. One worker escaped injury.

The derailment of an eastbound Burlington Northern coal train killed conductor E. F. "Ed" Stewart, who was riding in the caboose.

# The Lemberger Collection

The accident, which also injured another worker, happened four miles west of Albia, Iowa on June 27, 1977.

Demolition and salvage of the Milwaukee Railroad freight depot, located under the Jefferson Street viaduct, in August 1977.

# The Lemberger Collection

Commonly known as the Freight House, the building had not been used in several years.

Cleaning the signal lights at the Market Street crossing, Ottumwa, in October 1978.

## The Lemberger Collection

Cleaning up a 1,400-gallon diesel oil spill on the Milwakuee Railroad near Bear Creek, January 5, 1979.

Rock Island switch engine between Market Street and Green Street in Ottumwa, taken in March 1975.

# The Lemberger Collection

Coal cars derailed from a Burlington Northern freight east of Ottumwa in February, 1978.

# Railroads of Southeast Iowa

Burlington Railroad switching yard in Ottumwa's east end, west of Iowa Avenue near the Morrell meatpacking plant, in November 1977.

Milwaukee yards in downtown Ottumwa, just east of Market Street.
No longer used by 1982.

# The Lemberger Collection

Repairing Burlington Northern tracks near Market Street
in Ottumwa, September 1978.

Milwaukee Railroad roundhouse, in the yards west of Ottumwa near Wildwood Drive, about to be torn down -- March 1979.

# The Lemberger Collection

More than 300 men were employed here, operating around the clock seven days a week. The roundhouse included a machine shop and foundry where workers made many parts for steam locomotives.

Buildings in the Milwaukee Railroad yards west of Ottumwa near Wildwood Drive, torn down in March 1979.

The building at center housed the office of the roundhouse foreman, a position held for many years by Harold Hill.

# The Lemberger Collection

Wabash bridge over the Des Moines River, Ottumwa, July 1982.

# The Lemberger Collection

Looking east toward the Eldon, Iowa depot (Wapello County) in 1982.

Wabash bridge over the Des Moines River, Ottumwa, July 1982.

## Railroads of Southeast Iowa

Milwaukee engineer Dick Graham in the cab of a freight locomotive at the end of a strike by railroad engineers -- September 23, 1982.

# Railroads of Southeast Iowa

Amtrak F-40 locomotive #300, photographed in June 1982.

## The Lemberger Collection

A 1980 bomb threat to Amtrak's Superliner caused a long stopover in Ottumwa while the train was searched. No bomb was found.

Amtrak dining car in 1984, when cloth napkins were in use.

An empty coal train speeding westward toward downtown Ottumwa, seen from the pedestrian walkway over the tracks at Iowa Avenue (near the former site of the Morrell meatpacking plant) in October 1981.

# The Lemberger Collection

Burlington Northern freight headed east toward the Jefferson Street viaduct.

Cleaning switches in the snow.

# The Lemberger Collection

Waiting for the crossing to clear at Market Street, Ottumwa -- July 1982.

Burlington Northern FP-45 locomotive # 6635,
near the Market Street parking lot, October 1981.

```
E-11-84  1800 PADS                    FORM 214 REV.
        Chicago, Milwaukee, St. Paul and Pacific Railroad Company
                              CLEARANCE
                                                      ,            19
STATION
To
```

# The Lemberger Collection

A crew found a unique coat rack while repairing the crossing on the Milwaukee track in Marina Gateway in April, 1983.

The depot at Eldon, Iowa after the tracks were removed -- February 1983.

# The Lemberger Collection

BNSF tracks near the Eldon Y on Highway 34, looking west at sunset.

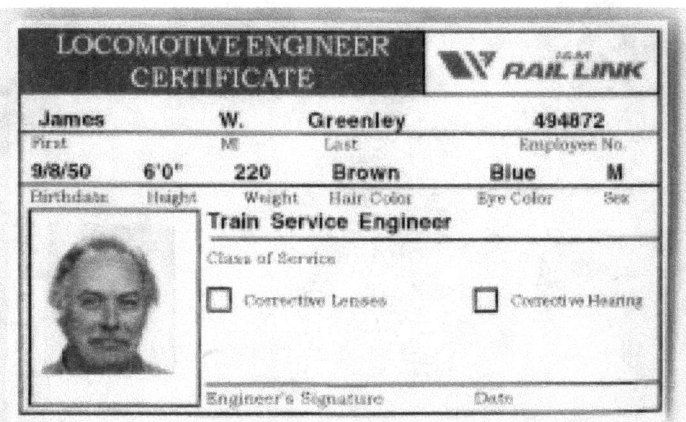

Empty ribbon rail train just east of the Jefferson Street viaduct.

Ringling Brothers & Barnum & Bailey circus train (the red train) at Nahant (near Davenport, Iowa) August 20, 1991. *(Photo by Mark Zaputil).*

Burlington Northern caboose on display at Melrose, Iowa (Monroe County).

Amtrak train #5 arriving in Ottumwa on July 21, 2011.

# The Lemberger Collection

For more information about these and other books, calendars and products, visit
**www.pbllimited.com**
PBL Limited
P.O. Box 935
Ottumwa Iowa 52501

www.ingramcontent.com/pod-product-compliance
Lightning Source LLC
Chambersburg PA
CBHW080246170426
43192CB00014BA/2582